PHRASEBOOK
RUSSIAN

GW00802221

PHRASEBOOK
RUSSIAN

AA

English edition prepared by First Edition Translations Ltd,
Great Britain
Designed and produced by AA Publishing
First published in 1995 as Wat & Hoe Russisch,
© Uitgeverij Kosmos bv - Utrecht/Antwerpen
Van Dale Lexicografie bv - Utrecht/Antwerpen
This edition © Automobile Association Developments Limited 2006
Reprinted September 2008

A CIP catalogue record for this book is available from the
British Library.

Published by AA Publishing (a trading name of Automobile
Association Developments Limited, whose registered office is
Fanum House, Basingstoke, Hampshire RG21 4EA.
Registered number 1878835).

Typeset by Kate Harling.
Printed and bound in China by Everbest.

Find out more about AA Publishing by visiting our website at
www.theAA.com/bookshop

A03953

Contents

Introduction 6
Pronunciation table 7

1 Useful lists 9–23

1.1	Today or tomorrow? 10	**1.6**	Here, there ... 19
1.2	Bank holidays 12	**1.7**	What does that sign say? 21
1.3	What time is it? 12		
1.4	One, two, three ... 14	**1.8**	Telephone alphabet 22
1.5	The weather 17	**1.9**	Personal details 23

2 Courtesies 24–32

2.1	Greetings 25	**2.4**	Thank you 30
2.2	How to ask a question 26	**2.5**	Sorry 30
2.3	How to reply 29	**2.6**	What do you think? 31

3 Conversation 33–47

3.1	I beg your pardon? 34	**3.6**	Hobbies 41
3.2	Introductions 35	**3.7**	Being the host(ess) 41
3.3	Starting/ending a conversation 39	**3.8**	Invitations 42
		3.9	Paying a compliment 43
3.4	Congratulations and condolences 40	**3.10**	Chatting someone up 44
		3.11	Arrangements 46
3.5	A chat about the weather 40	**3.12**	Saying goodbye 46

4 Eating out 48–62

4.1	On arrival 49	**4.5**	Paying a compliment 57
4.2	Ordering 51	**4.6**	The menu 57
4.3	The bill 55	**4.7**	Alphabetical list of drinks and dishes 58
4.4	Complaints 55		

5 On the road 63–80

5.1	Asking for directions 64	**5.6**	The petrol station 70
5.2	Customs 65	**5.7**	Breakdown and repairs 74
5.3	Luggage 68	**5.8**	The bicycle/moped 76
5.4	Traffic signs 69		*The parts of a bicycle* 78
5.5	The car 70	**5.9**	Renting a vehicle 77
	The parts of a car 72	**5.10**	Hitchhiking 80

6 Public transport 81–92

6.1	In general 82	**6.4**	Information 88
6.2	Questions to passengers 84	**6.5**	Aeroplanes 90
6.3	Tickets 86	**6.6**	Taxis 91

7 Overnight accommodation 93–104

7.1	General 94	**7.3**	Hotel/B&B/apartment/ holiday house 100
7.2	Camping 95	**7.4**	Complaints 102
	Camping equipment 98	**7.5**	Departure 104

8 Money matters 105–108

8.1	Banks 106	**8.2**	Settling the bill 107

9 Post and telephone 109–114

9.1	Post 110	**9.2**	Telephone 112

10   Shopping 115–127

10.1 Shopping
conversations 116
10.2 Food 119
10.3 Clothing and shoes 120

10.4 Photographs
and video 122
10.5 At the hairdresser's 125

11   At the Tourist Information Centre 128–134

11.1 Places of interest 129
11.2 Going out 131

11.3 Booking tickets 133

12   Sports 135–138

12.1 Sporting questions 136
12.2 By the waterfront 136

12.3 In the snow 138

13   Sickness 139–148

13.1 Call (fetch) the doctor 140
13.2 Patient's ailments 140
13.3 The consultation 142

13.4 Medication and
prescriptions 146
13.5 At the dentist's 147

14   In trouble 149–156

14.1 Asking for help 150
14.2 Loss 151
14.3 Accidents 152

14.4 Theft 153
14.5 Missing person 153
14.6 The police 154

15   Word list 157–220

Word list English – Russian 158

Basic grammar 221–224

Basic grammar 222

Introduction

● **Welcome to the AA's essential Phrase Books series**, covering the most popular European languages and containing everything you'd expect from a comprehensive language series. They're concise, accessible and easy to understand, and you'll find them indispensable on your trip abroad.

Each guide is divided into 15 themed sections and starts with a pronunciation table which gives you the phonetic spelling to all the words and phrases you'll need to know for your trip, while at the back of the book is an extensive word list and grammar guide which will help you construct basic sentences in your chosen language.

Throughout the book you'll come across coloured boxes with a [image] beside them. These are designed to help you if you can't understand what your listener is saying to you. Hand the book over to them and encourage them to point to the appropriate answer to the question you are asking.

Other coloured boxes in the book – this time without the symbol — give alphabetical listings of themed words with their English translations beside them.

For extra clarity, we have put all English words and phrases in black, foreign language terms in red and their phonetic pronunciation in italic.

This phrase book covers all subjects you are likely to come across during the course of your visit, from reserving a room for the night to ordering food and drink at a restaurant and what to do if your car breaks down or you lose your traveller's cheques and money. With over 2,000 commonly used words and essential phrases at your fingertips you can rest assured that you will be able to get by in all situations, so let the essential Phrase Book become your passport to a secure and enjoyable trip!

Pronunciation table

The most important thing about the pronunciation of Russian words is their stress. Each Russian word longer than one syllable has one main stress, so getting the stress right maximises the chances of the person you are talking to recognising the word you are saying. In this phrasebook the stressed syllable is indicated in bold type in the English transcription. Occasionally you will see a word of only one syllable stressed: this conveys meaning to the whole sentence, for instance turning it from a statement into a question.

Sounds

The Russian words in this phrasebook have been transcribed in a way that is as close to the look of English words as possible. In order to imitate some special Russian sounds, in our transcription we have used the following conventions:

kh is pronounced as **ch** in Scottish **loch**
air is pronounced as in **fair**
igh is pronounced as in **high**
or when followed by a hyphen has a silent **r**
zh is pronounced like the **s** in **treasure**
y when not followed by a vowel stands for the unique Russian vowel
ō (see Russian alphabet on next page)

The Russian alphabet

А	а	long, as in **father**
Б	б	**b** as in **book**
В	в	**v** as in **vote**
Г	г	**g** as in **good**
Д	д	**d** as in **day**
Е	е	**yeh** as in **yell**
Ё	ё	**yoh** as in **yonder**
Ж	ж	**s** as in **treasure**
З	з	**z** as in **zone**
И	и	**ee** as in **meet**
Й	й	**y** as in **boy**
К	к	**k** as in **kind**
Л	л	**l** as in **look**
М	м	**m** as in **man**
Н	н	**n** as in **note**
О	о	long, as in **port**
П	п	**p** as in **pen**
Р	р	**r** rolled as in **Rory**
С	с	**s** as in **speak**
Т	т	**t** as in **too**
У	у	**oo** as in **oodles**
Ф	ф	**f** as in fire
Х	х	**ch** as in Scottish **loch**
Ц	ц	**ts** as in **carts**
Ч	ч	**ch** as in **cheep**
Ш	ш	**sh** as in **short**
Щ	щ	**shch** as in **pushchair**
	ъ	**hard** sign, not pronounced
	ы	very **hard i** as in **igloo**
	ь	**soft** sign, not pronounced
Э	э	**e** as in **men**
Ю	ю	**yu** as in **Yukon**
Я	я	**ya** as in **yard**

1 Useful lists

1.1 Today or tomorrow? 10

1.2 Bank holidays 12

1.3 What time is it? 12

1.4 One, two, three... 14

1.5 The weather 17

1.6 Here, there... 19

1.7 What does that sign say? 21

1.8 Telephone alphabet 22

1.9 Personal details 23

1.1 Today or tomorrow?

What day is it today? _____	**Какой сегодня день?**
	Kakoy sivordnya dyen?
Today's Monday _____	**Сегодня понедельник**
	Sivordnya punidyelneek
– Tuesday _____	**вторник**
	ftorneek
– Wednesday _____	**среда**
	sridar
– Thursday _____	**четверг**
	chitvyairk
– Friday _____	**пятница**
	pyatnitsa
– Saturday _____	**суббота**
	sooborta
– Sunday_____	**воскресенье**
	vuskrisyaynya
in January_____	**в январе**
	vyanvaryeh
since February_____	**с февраля**
	sfevralya
in spring _____	**весной**
	visnoy
in summer_____	**летом**
	lyetum
in autumn _____	**осенью**
	orsinyu
in winter _____	**зимой**
	zeemoy
1997 _____	**тысяча девятьсот девяносто седьмой год**
	tysicha divutsort divyanorsta sidmoy gort
the twentieth century ____	**двадцатый век**
	dvutsarty vyek

What's the date today? __	**Какое сегодня число?**
	Kakoya sivordnya cheesslor?
Today's the 23rd _____	**Сегодня двадцать третье**
	Sivordnya dvartsut tryaytyeh
Monday 2 November ____ 1998	**понедельник, второе ноября тысяча девятьсот девяносто восьмого года**
	punidyelneek, fturroyeh nuyubbrya tysicha divutsort divyanorsta vussmorva gorda
in the morning _____	**утром** *ootrum*
in the afternoon _____	**днём** *dnyom*
in the evening _____	**вечером** *vaychirum*
at night _____	**ночью**
	norchyu
this morning_____	**сегодня утром**
	sivordnya ootrum
this afternoon_____	**сегодня днём**
	sivordnya dnyom
this evening _____	**сегодня вечером**
	sivordnya vaychirum
tonight_____	**сегодня ночью**
	sivordnya norchyu
last night_____	**прошлой ночью**
	prorshloy norchyu
this week _____	**на этой неделе**
	na etoy nidyaylye
next month_____	**в следующем месяце**
	fslyedooyushchem myaysyetseh
last year _____	**в прошлом году**
	vprorshlum guddoo
next... _____	**следующий...**
	slyedooyushchee...
in...days/weeks/ _____ months/years	**через...дней/недель/месяцев/лет** *chayruss...dnyay/nidyell/myaysyetsev/lyet*
...weeks ago_____	**...недель тому назад**
	...nidyell tummoo nazat
day off_____	**выходной день**
	vykhudnoy dyen

11

1.2 Bank holidays

● **The most important** national ('Bank') holidays in Russia are:

1 January	New Year (Новый Год, *Norvy Gort*)
8 March	International Women's Day (Международный женский день, *Myezhdoonarordny zhenski dyen*)
1 May	May Day (Праздник Первого Мая, *Prarznik pyairvuvva mighya*)
9 May	Victory Day (День Победы, *Dyen Pubbyedy*)
12 June	Independence Day (День независимости России, *Dyen nyezaveessimusti Russee-ee*)

On these days, banks and government institutions are closed.
Religious festivals are also being increasingly observed.
The Russian Orthodox Church still follows the Julian Calendar, which is thirteen days behind the Western Gregorian calendar. The most important Russian Orthodox festivals are:

Christmas	7 January (Рождество, *Ruzhdistvor*)
Easter	May coincide with Western Easter, (Пасха, *Parskha*), be one week later, or five weeks later
Ascension Day	Forty days after Easter (Вознесение, *Vuznisyayniya*)
Whitsun	Fifty days after Easter (Троицын день, *Troyitsin dyen*)

1.3 What time is it?

What time is it? _____	**Который час?** *Kutory chass?*
It's nine o'clock _____	**Девять часов** *Dyevit chassorf*
– five past ten _____	**Десять часов пять минут** *Dyesit chassorf pyat minoot*
– a quarter past eleven __	**Одиннадцать часов пятнадцать минут** *Udeenatsat chassorf pitnatsat minoot*

– twenty past twelve	**Двенадцать часов двадцать минут**
	Dvinartsat chassorf dvartsat minoot
– half past one	**Половина второго**
	Puluvveena fturorva
– twenty–five to three	**Без двадцати пяти три**
	Byes dvutsutee pitee tree
– a quarter to four	**Без четверти четыре**
	Byes chaytvertee chiteery
– ten to five	**Без десяти пять**
	Byes disyatee pyat
– twelve noon	**Двенадцать часов дня**
	Dvinartsut chassorf dnya
– midnight	**Двенадцать часов ночи**
	Dvinartsut chassorf norchi
half an hour	**полчаса**
	polchassah
What time?	**В котором часу?**
	Fkutorum chassoo?
What time can I come round?	**В котором часу мне прийти?**
	Fkutorum chassoo mnyeh preetee?
At...	**В...**
	V...
After...	**После...**
	Porslyeh...
Before...	**До...**
	Dor...
Between...and...	**Между...и...**
	Myezhdoo...ee...
From...to...	**С...до...**
	S...dor...
In...minutes	**Через...минут**
	Chayruss...minoot
– ...hours	**Через...часов**
	Chayruss...chassorf
– a quarter of an hour	**Через четверть часа**
	Chayruss chaytvert chassah

– three quarters of _____ an hour	**Через сорок пять минут**	*Chayruss soruk pyat minoot*
early/late _____	**Слишком рано/поздно**	*Sleeshkum rarno/porzna*
on time _____	**вовремя**	*vorvremya*
summertime _____	**летнее время**	*lyetnyeya vraymya*
wintertime _____	**зимнее время**	*zeemnyeya vraymya*

1.4 One, two, three...

0 _____	**ноль/нуль**	*norl/nool*
1 _____	**один**	*udeen*
2 _____	**два**	*dvah*
3 _____	**три**	*tree*
4 _____	**четыре**	*chiteery*
5 _____	**пять**	*pyat*
6 _____	**шесть**	*shest*
7 _____	**семь**	*syem*
8 _____	**восемь**	*vorsim*
9 _____	**девять**	*dyevit*
10 _____	**десять**	*dyesit*
11 _____	**одиннадцать**	*udeenatsut*
12 _____	**двенадцать**	*dvinartsut*
13 _____	**тринадцать**	*trinartsut*
14 _____	**четырнадцать**	*chiteernatsut*
15 _____	**пятнадцать**	*pitnartsut*
16 _____	**шестнадцать**	*shistnartsut*
17 _____	**семнадцать**	*simnartsut*
18 _____	**восемнадцать**	*vusimnartsut*
19 _____	**девятнадцать**	*divitnartsut*
20 _____	**двадцать**	*dvartsut*
21 _____	**двадцать один**	*dvartsut udeen*

22 _____	двадцать два	*dvartsut dvah*
30 _____	тридцать	*treetsut*
31 _____	тридцать один	*treetsut udeen*
32 _____	тридцать два	*treetsut dvah*
40 _____	сорок	*soruk*
50 _____	пятьдесят	*pitdisyaht*
60 _____	шестьдесят	*shistdisyaht*
70 _____	семьдесят	*syemdisyut*
80 _____	восемьдесят	*vorsimdisyut*
90 _____	девяносто	*divyanorsto*
100 _____	сто	*stor*
101 _____	сто один	*stor udeen*
110 _____	сто десять	*stor dyesit*
120 _____	сто двадцать	*stor dvartsut*
200 _____	двести	*dvyaysti*
300 _____	триста	*treesta*
400 _____	четыреста	*chiteerista*
500 _____	пятьсот	*pitsort*
600 _____	шестьсот	*shistsort*
700 _____	семьсот	*simsort*
800 _____	восемьсот	*vusimsort*
900 _____	девятьсот	*divutsort*
1000 _____	тысяча	*tysicha*
1100 _____	тысяча сто	*tysicha stor*
2000 _____	две тысячи	*dvyeh tysichi*
10,000 _____	десять тысяч	*dyesit tysich*
100,000 _____	сто тысяч	*stor tysich*
1,000,000 _____	миллион	*meeliorn*
1st _____	первый	*pyairvy*
2nd _____	второй	*fturoy*
3rd _____	третий	*traytyee*
4th _____	чевёртый	*chitvyorty*
5th _____	пятый	*pyarty*
6th _____	шестой	*shistoy*
7th _____	седьмой	*sidmoy*
8th _____	восьмой	*vusmoy*

9th _____	**девятый**	*divyahty*
10th _____	**десятый**	*disyahty*
11th _____	**одиннадцатый**	*udeenatsuty*
12th _____	**двенадцатый**	*dvinartsuty*
13th _____	**тринадцатый**	*trinartsuty*
14th _____	**четырнадцатый**	*chityrnatsuty*
15th _____	**пятнадцатый**	*pitnartsuty*
16th _____	**шестнадцатый**	*shistnartsuty*
17th _____	**семнадцатый**	*simnartsuty*
18th _____	**восемнадцатый**	*vusimnartsuty*
19th _____	**девятнадцатый**	*divitnartsuty*
20th _____	**двадцатый**	*dvutsarty*
21st _____	**двадцать первый**	*dvartsut pyairvy*
22nd _____	**двадцать второй**	*dvartsut fturoy*
30th _____	**тридцатый**	*tritsarty*
100th _____	**сотый**	*sorty*
1000th _____	**тысячный**	*tysichny*

once _____	**раз**	
	rass	
twice _____	**дважды**	
	dvarzhdy	
double _____	**вдвойне**	
	vdvoynyeh	
triple _____	**втройне**	
	vtroynyeh	
half _____	**половина**	
	puluvveena	
a quarter _____	**четверть**	
	chaytvert	
a third _____	**треть**	
	trayt	
a couple, a few, some ___	**несколько**	
	nyeskulka	

2+4=6 _____	два плюс четыре равняется шести
	dvah plyus chiteery ravnyaitsa shistee
4-2=2_____	четыре минус два равняется двум
	chiteery meenus dvah ravnyaitsa dvoom
2x4=8_____	два на четыре равняется восьми
	dvah na chiteery ravnyaitsa vusmee
4÷2=2_____	четыре разделить на два равняется
	двум
	chiteery razdeleet na dvah ravnyaitsa
	dvoom
odd/even _____	чётно/нечётно
	chotna/nichotna
total _____	в итоге
	veetorgyeh
6x9_____	шесть на девять
	shest na dyevit

1.5 The weather

Is the weather going_____ to be good/bad?	Будет хорошая/плохая погода?
	Boodyetkhurorshaya/plukhaya pugorda?
Is it going to get _____ colder/hotter?	Похолодает?/Потеплеет?
	Pukhulludighet?/Puttiplayet?
What temperature is it ___ going to be?	Сколько будет градусов?
	Skorlka boodyet grahdoosoff?
Is it going to rain?_____	Будет дождь?
	Boodyet dorzht?
Is there going to be a____ storm?	Будет буря?
	Boodyet boorya?
Is it going to snow? _____	ПойдСт снег?
	Puydyot snyek?
Is it going to freeze?_____	Будет мороз?
	Boodyet murorss?
Is the thaw setting in? ___	Будет оттепель?
	Boodyet ort-tipyel?

Is it going to be foggy? __	**Будет туман?**	
	Boodyet toomarn?	
Is there going to be a ____ thunderstorm?	**Будет гроза?**	
	Boodyet gruzzah?	
The weather's changing __	**Погода меняется**	
	Pugorda minyayetsa	
It's cooling down _____	**Холодает**	
	Khullud-eye-yet	
What's the weather _____ going to be like today/ tomorrow?	**Какая будет сегодня/завтра погода?**	
	Kakaya boodyet sivordnya/zarftra pugorda?	

погода	**солнечно**	**временами**
weather	sunny	occasionally
мороз	**град**	**максимальная/мини**
frost	hail	**мальнаятемперату**
безоблачно	**сыро**	**ра около**
clear	wet	maximum/minimum
облачно	**дождь**	temperature
cloudy	rain	about
ветер	**тепло**	**временами**
wind	warm	**дождь/снег**
прохладно	**душно**	occasionally rain/snow
cool	close	**облачная погода с**
ветрено	**туман**	**прояснениями**
windy	fog	cloudy with clear
свежо	**(очень) жарко**	intervals
fresh	(very) hot	**северный/восточны**
сильный ветер	**(очень) холодно**	**й/южный/**
strong wind	(very) cold	**западный ветер**
снег	**...градусов**	winds
snow	**ниже/выше нуля**	northerly/easterly/
гололедица	...degrees	southerly/westerly
black ice	below/above zero	

1.6 Here, there...

See also 5.1 Asking for directions

here/there _____	**здесь/там**
	zdyess/tarm
somewhere/nowhere _____	**где-то/нигде**
	gdyeh-ta/neegdyeh
everywhere_____	**везде**
	vyizdyeh
far away/nearby_____	**далеко/близко**
	dalikor/bleeska
right/left_____	**направо/налево**
	nuprarva/nulyeva
to the right/left of _____	**справа/слева от**
	sprarva/slyeva ut
straight ahead _____	**прямо**
	pryarma
via _____	**через**
	chayruss
in _____	**в**
	v
on_____	**на**
	nah
under_____	**под**
	pudd
against _____	**против**
	prorteef
opposite _____	**напротив**
	nahprorteef
next to_____	**возле**
	vorzlyeh
near _____	**у**
	oo
in front of _____	**перед**
	pyayrut

English	Russian	Transliteration
in the centre	в середине	*fsirideenyeh*
forward	вперёд	*fpiryot*
at the bottom	внизу	*vneezoo*
down/downwards	вниз	*vneess*
at the top	наверху	*navirkhoo*
up/upwards	наверх	*nuvyairkh*
inside	внутри	*vnootree*
into the inside	внутрь	*vnootr*
on the outside	снаружи	*snaroozhy*
from behind	сзади	*s-zardee*
back/ago	назад	*nuzzaht*
at the front	впереди	*vpiridee*
at the back	позади	*puzzudee*
in the north	на севере	*nah sayveeryeh*
to the south	на юг	*nah yook*
from the west	с запада	*s-zarpudda*
from the east	с востока	*s-vustorka*
to the...of	на...от	*nah...ort...*

администрация
manager

купаться воспрещается
swimming prohibited

вода не для питья
no drinking water

лестница stairs

вход
entrance

лифт
lift

вход бесплатный/ свободный
free admission

место для инвалидов и пассажиров с детьми
These seats are reserved for disabled persons or passengers with children

высокое напряжение
high voltage

выход
exit

мужской туалет
gents/gentlemen

20

1.7 What does that sign say?

See also 5.4 Traffic signs

женский туалет
ladies

не беспокоить
do not disturb

заказано
reserved

не влезай, убьёт
keep out: danger to
life

закрыт на обед
closed for lunch

не высовываться
do not lean out

закрыт на
(капитальный)
ремонт
closed for (major)
repairs

не курить no smoking

запасный выход
emergency exit

не работает
out of order

запасный тормоз
emergency brake

не трогать
please do not touch

запрещено
разжигать костёр
no open fires

огнеопасно
fire hazard

запрещено для
домашних
животных
no pets allowed

опасно danger

осторожно caution

информация
information

осторожно, злая
собака
beware of the dog

к поездам
to the trains

осторожно,
окрашено
wet paint

к себе/от себя
pull/push

открыто/закрыто
open/closed

касса pay here

питьевая вода
drinking water

платформа
platform

свободных мест
нет
full/sold out/no
vacancies

по газону не ходить
keep off the grass

сдаётся в наём
for hire

пожарная
лестница
fire escape

смертельно
опасно
danger to life

посторонним вход
воспрещён
no entry

фотографировать
воспрещается
no photographs

продаётся
for sale

частная
собственность
private property

путь
track (platform)

частное владение
no trespassing

рабочее время
opening hours

регистратура
escalator

эскалатор
reception

этаж
floor

1.8 Telephone alphabet

а	*(ah)*	как Анна	*kukk Arna*
б	*(beh)*	как Борис	*kukk Burreess*
в	*(veh)*	как Виктор	*kukk Veektur*
г	*(geh)*	как Григорий	*kukk Greegoree*
д	*(deh)*	как Дмитрий	*kukk Dmeetree*
е	*(yeh)*	как Елена	*kukk Yelyayna*
ё	*(yoh)*	как Ёлка	*kukk Yolka*
ж	*(zheh)*	как Женя	*kukk Zhenya*
з	*(zeh)*	как Зоя	*kukk Zoy-ya*
и	*(ee)*	как Ирина	*kukk Ireena*
й	*(ee krartkoye)*	как Йод	*kukk Yot*
к	*(kah)*	как Константин	*kukk Kunstanteen*
л	*(ell)*	как Лиза	*kukk Leeza*
м	*(em)*	как Мария	*kukk Murreeya*
н	*(en)*	как Наташа	*kukk Nutarsha*
о	*(or)*	как Ольга	*kukk Orlga*
п	*(peh)*	как Пётр	*kukk Pyotr*
р	*(air)*	как Руслан	*kukk Roosslarn*
с	*(ess)*	как Семён	*kukk Simyon*
т	*(teh)*	как Татьяна	*kukk Tuteeyarna*
у	*(oo)*	как Украина	*kukk Ookraeena*
ф	*(eff)*	как Фёдор	*kukk Fyodur*
х	*(khah)*	как Харьков	*kukk Kharkuff*
ц	*(tseh)*	как Царица	*kukk Tsareetsa*
ч	*(cheh)*	как Чехов	*kukk Chekhuff*
ш	*(shah)*	как Шура	*kukk Shoora*
щ	*(shchah)*	как Щука	*kukk Shchooka*
ъ	*(tvyordy znark)*		
ы	*(y)*	} not used at beginning of word	
ь	*(myarkhki znark)*		
э	*(eh)*	как Эрик	*kukk Aireek*
ю	*(yoo)*	как Юрий	*kukk Yooree*
я	*(yah)*	как Яна	*kukk Yahna*

1.9 Personal details

Russians have a single forename and a surname, and in between a name that is derived from their father's forename (the so-called patronymic). For example:

Пётр Иванович Кузнецов

Pyotr Ivarnovich Kooznitsorff

Анна Петровна Кузнецова

Arna Pitrorvna Kooznitsorva

The patronymic is most often used preceded by the forename as a polite form of address.

surname _____	**фамилия** *fameeliya*
forename_____	**имя** *eemya*
patronymic _____	**отчество** *ortchistva*
initials _____	**инициалы** *initseearly*
address (street/number)__	**адрес (улица/дом)**
	ardriss (ooleetsa/dorm)
post code/town _____	**индекс/местожительство**
	eendiks/myestozheetelstva
sex (male/female) _____	**пол (м/ж)** *porl (m/zh)*
nationality _____	**национальность** *nutsiunarlnust*
date of birth _____	**дата рождения** *darta ruzhdyayniya*
place of birth _____	**место рождения** *myesta ruzhdyayniya*
occupation _____	**профессия** *pruffaysiya*
married/single/divorced __	**женат (замужем) / не женат (не**
(bracketed form when	**замужем)/ разведен (разведена)**
woman speaking)	*zhinart(zarmoozhum) /nyeh zhinart (nyeh*
	zarmooozhum) /ruzvidyon (ruzvidyinar)
widowed m/f _____	**вдовец/вдова** *vduvyets/vduvvar*
(number of) children _____	**дети** *dyayti*
passport/identity _____	**номер паспорта / номер водительских**
card/driving licence	**прав**
number	*normir parssporta / normir vudeetyilskeekh*
	prahff
place and date of issue __	**место и дата выдачи**
	myesta ee darta vyduchi

2 Courtesies

2.1 Greetings 25

2.2 How to ask a question 26

2.3 How to reply 29

2.4 Thank you 30

2.5 Sorry 30

2.6 What do you think? 31

2.1 Greetings

Hello, Mr Smith _____	**Здравствуйте, господин Смит** *Zdrarstvootyeh, guspuddeen Smeet*
Hello, Mrs Jones _____	**Здравствуйте, госпожа Джонс** *Zdrarstvootyeh, guspuzhar Dzhorns*
Hello, Peter _____	**Привет, Питер** *Preevyet, Peetir*
Hi, Helen_____	**Привет, Хелен** *Preevyet, Khelin*
Good morning, madam __	**Доброе утро, госпожа** *Dorbroya ootra, guspuzhar*
Good afternoon, sir _____	**Добрый день, господин** *Dorbry dyen, guspuddeen*
Good evening _____	**Добрый вечер** *Dorbry vaychir*
How are you? _____ How's things?	**Как поживаете? Как дела?** *Kukk puzhivahyetyeh? Kukk dillar?*
Fine, thank you, _____ and you?	**Хорошо, а вы?** *Khurushor, ah vy?*
Very well _____	**Отлично** *Utleechna*
Not very well _____	**Не очень** *Nyeh orchin*
Not too bad _____	**Ничего** *Nichivor*
I'd better be going _____	**Я, пожалуй, пойду** *Ya, puzharlooy, puydoo*

I have to be going_____
  Someone's waiting
  for me
	Я должен идти. Меня ждут.
	Ya dorlzhun eed-tee. Minya zhdoot

Bye! _____	**Пока!** *Pukkah!*
Goodbye_____	**До свидания** *Duh svidarniya*

See you soon_____	**До скорого**
	Duh skorova
See you in a little while/__ cheerio	**Пока**
	Pukkah
Sleep well_____	**Спокойной ночи**
	Spukkoyny norchee
Good night_____	**Доброй ночи**
	Dorbry norchee
All the best_____	**Всего наилучшего**
	Vsivor na-eeloochshiva
Have fun _____	**Всего хорошего**
	Vsivor khororshiva
Good luck_____	**Удачи**
	Oodarchee
Have a nice holiday _____	**Хорошего отдыха**
	Khurorshiva ortdykha
Have a good trip_____	**Счастливого пути**
	Schastleevuvva pootee
Thank you, you too_____	**Спасибо, вам того же**
	Spaseeba, varm tuvvor zheh
Say hello to...for me _____	**Привет...**
	Preevyet...

2.2 How to ask a question

Who?_____	**Кто?**
	Ktor?
Who's that? _____	**Кто это?**
	Ktor eta?
What? _____	**Что?**
	Shtor?
What's there to _____ see here?	**Что здесь можно посмотреть?**
	Shtor zdyess morzhna pusmutrayt?

What kind of hotel_____ is that?	**Что это за гостиница?** *Shtor eta zah gusteenitsa?*
Where? _____	**Где?** *Gdyeh?*
Where's the toilet? _____	**Где туалет?** *Gdyeh too-alyet?*
Where are you going? ___	**Куда вы идёте?** *Koodar by eedyotye?*
Where are you from? ____	**Откуда вы?** *Utkoodah vy?*
How?_____	**Как?** *Kark?*
How far is that?_____	**Как это далеко?** *Kukk eta dalikor?*
How long does that take?	**Сколько это длится?** *Skorlka eta dleetsa?*
How long is the trip? ____	**Сколько длится путешествие?** *Skorlka dleetsa pootyeshestviya?*
How much? _____	**Сколько?** *Skorlka?*
How much is this? _____	**Сколько это стоит?** *Skorlka eta stor-eet?*
What time is it? _____	**Который час?** *Kutory chass?*
Which one? _____ Which ones?	**Который? Которые?** *Kutory? Kutory-yeh?*
Which glass is mine? ____	**Которая рюмка для меня?** *Kutoraya ryoomka dlya minya?*
When?_____	**Когда?** *Kugdar?*
When are you leaving?___	**Когда вы уезжаете?** *Kugdar vy oo-yizhah-yityeh?*
Why? _____	**Почему?** *Puchimoo?*
Could you...me? _____	**Не могли бы вы...?** *Nyeh muglee by vy...?*

Could you help me, _____ please?	**Не могли бы вы мне помочь?** *Nyeh muglee by vy mnyeh pummorch?*
Could you point that_____ out to me?	**Не могли бы вы мне показать?** *Nyeh muglee by vy mnyeh pukkuzzart?*
Could you come _____ with me, please?	**Не могли бы вы пойти со мной?** *Nyeh muglee by vy puytee sumnoy?*
Could you... _____	**Вы можете...?** *Vy morzhityeh...?*
Could you reserve some _ tickets for me, please?	**Вы можете заказать для меня билеты?** *Vy morzhityeh zukkuzzart dlya minya bilyety?*
Do you know...? _____	**Вы знаете...?** *Vy znahyityeh...?*
Do you know another_____ hotel, please?	**Вы не знаете другую гостиницу?** *Vy nyeh znahyityeh droogooyu gusteenitsoo?*
Do you have a...? _____	**У вас есть...?** *Oo vass yest...?*
Do you have a _____ vegetarian dish, please?	**Есть у вас что-нибудь вегетарианское?** *Yest oo vass shtor-neeboot vegetariarnskoya?*
I'd like... _____	**Мне...,пожалуйста** *Mnyeh...,puzharlooysta*
I'd like a kilo of apples, _ please.	**Мне килограмм яблок, пожалуйста** *Mnyeh keelugrahm yabluk, puzharlooysta*
Can I...? _____	**Можно...?** *Morzhna...?*
Can I take this? _____	**Можно это забрать?** *Morzhna eta zubbrart?*
Can I smoke here? _____	**Здесь можно курить?** *Zdyess morzhno kooreet?*
Could I ask you _____ something?	**Можно вас спросить?** *Morzhno vass sprusseet?*

2.3 How to reply

Yes, of course _____	**Да, конечно**
	*Dah, kun**ye**shna*
No, I'm sorry _____	**Нет, извините**
	*Nyet, eezvin**ee**tyeh*
Yes, what can I do _____ for you?	**Да, что я могу для вас сделать?**
	*D**ah**, shto yah mug**goo** dlya vass zd**yell**at?*
Just a moment, please __	**Одну минуту, пожалуйста**
	*Udn**oo** min**oo**too, puzhar**loo**ysta*
No, I don't have _____ time now	**Нет, мне некогда**
	*Nyet, mnyeh n**yay**kugda*
No, that's impossible ____	**Нет, это невозможно**
	Nyet, eta nivuzmorzhna
I think so _____	**Я думаю, да**
	*Ya d**oo**muyoo, dah*
I agree _____	**Я тоже так думаю**
	*Ya tor**zh**a tak d**oo**mayoo*
I hope so too _____	**Я тоже надеюсь**
	*Ya tor**zh**a nud**yey**us*
No, not at all _____	**Нет, совсем нет**
	*N**yet**, suvs**yem** nyet*
No, no one _____	**Нет, никто**
	*Nyet, neekt**or***
No, nothing _____	**Нет, ничего**
	*Nyet, nichivv**or***
That's (not) right _____	**Это правильно (неправильно)**
	*Eto pr**ar**veelna (nipr**ar**veelna)*
I (don't) agree _____	**Я с вами (не) согласен**
	*Ya sv**ar**mee (nyeh) sugg**lar**ssin*
All right _____	**Хорошо**
	*Khurush**or***
Okay _____	**Ладно** *Lardna*
Perhaps _____	**Может быть** *M**or**zhit byt*
I don't know _____	**Не знаю**
	*Nyeh zn**ah**-yu*

2.4 Thank you

Thank you_____	**Спасибо**
	Spaseeba
You're welcome_____	**Не за что**
	Nyeh za shto
Thank you very much____	**Огромное спасибо**
	Ugrormnaya spaseeba
Very kind of you _____	**Очень мило с вашей стороны**
	Orchin meela svarshay sturrunny
I enjoyed it very much ___	**Это доставило мне огромное**
	удовольствие
	Eto dustarveelo mnyeh urgrormnaya
	ooduvvorlstviyeh
Thank you for your _____	**Благодарю за беспокойство**
trouble	*Bluggudurryoo za byespukkoystva*
You shouldn't have _____	**Не нужно было этого делать**
	Nyeh noozhno byla etuvva dyelut
That's all right _____	**Всё в порядке**
	Vsyor fpuryatkyeh

2.5 Sorry

Excuse me _____	**Пардон**
	Pardorn
Sorry!_____	**Извините!**
	Eezvineetyeh!
I'm sorry, I didn't know..._	**Извините, я не знал (знала), что...**
	Eezvineetyeh, ya nyeh znarl
	(znarla), shtor...
I do apologise _____	**Простите меня**
	Prusteetyeh minya

I'm sorry _____	**Извините**
	Eezvineetyeh
I didn't do it on purpose,_ it was an accident	**Я не нарочно, это произошло случайно**
	Ya nyeh nurrorchna, eta pra-eezushlor sluchayna
That's all right _____	**Ничего страшного**
	Nichivvor strarshnuvva
Never mind_____	**Оставьте**
	Ustarvtyeh
It could've happened to__ anyone	**Со всяким может случиться**
	Sa fsyarkim morzhit sloocheetsa

2.6 What do you think?

Which do you prefer?____	**Что вы предпочитаете?**
	Shto vy pridpuchitah-yettyeh?
What do you think? _____	**Что ты об этом думаешь?**
	Shto ty ub etum doomuyesh?
Don't you like dancing? __	**Ты не любишь танцевать?**
	Ty nyeh lyoobish tuntsivart?
I don't mind _____	**Мне всё равно**
	Mnyeh fsyo ruvnor
Well done!_____	**Хорошо!**
	Khurushor!
Not bad! _____	**Неплохо!**
	Niplorkha!
Great! _____	**Великолепно!**
	Vileekulyepna!
Wonderful! _____	**Прекрасно!**
	Prikrarsno!
It's really nice here! _____	**Как здесь уютно!**
	Kukk zdyess oo-yootna!
How nice! _____	**Как здорово/красиво!**
	Kukk zdoruvva/krusseeva!

How nice for you! _____	**Как здорово для вас!**
	Kukk zdoruvva dlya vass!
I'm (not) very happy _____ with...	**Я (не) очень доволен (довольна) по поводу...**
	Ya (nyeh) orchin duvorlyin/duvorlna puh porvuddoo...
I'm glad... _____	**Я рад (рада), что...**
	Ya raht (rarda), shtor...
I'm having a great time __	**Я прекрасно провожу время**
	Ya prikrarsna pruvvuzhoo vraymya
I'm looking forward to it__	**Я заранее рад (рада)**
	Ya zurarnyehyeh raht (rarda)
I hope it'll work out_____	**Надеюсь, что это удастся**
	Nudyay-yus, shtor eta oodarstsa
That's ridiculous! _____	**Какая чушь!**
	Kukkahya choosh!
That's terrible! _____	**Как ужасно!**
	Kukk oozharsno!
What a pity! _____	**Как жаль!**
	Kukk zharl!
That's filthy! _____	**Как противно!**
	Kukk prutteevna!
What a load of rubbish! __	**Какая ерунда!**
	Kukkahya yiroondah!
I don't like... _____	**Я не люблю...**
	Ya nyeh lyooblyoo...
I'm bored to death _____	**Я ужасно скучаю**
	Ya oozharsno skoochahyoo
I've had enough _____	**Мне надоело**
	Mnye0h nuddayello
This is no good _____	**Так нельзя**
	Tukk nilzyah
I was expecting _____ something completely different	**Я ожидал (ожидала) совсем другого**
	Ya uzhidarl (uzhidarla) sufsyem droogorva

3 Conversation

3.1 I beg your pardon? 34

3.2 Introductions 35

3.3 Starting/ending a conversation 39

3.4 Congratulations and condolences 40

3.5 A chat about the weather 40

3.6 Hobbies 41

3.7 Being the host(ess) 41

3.8 Invitations 42

3.9 Paying a compliment 43

3.10 Chatting someone up 44

3.11 Arrangements 46

3.12 Saying goodbye 46

3.1 I beg your pardon?

I don't speak any/_____ I speak a little...	**Я не говорю по-.../Я немного говорю п-...** *Ya nyeh guvvuryoo puh.../Ya nimnorga guvvuryoo puh...*
I'm British _____	**Я из Великобритании** *Ya ees Vileekobritarnee-ee*
I'm English _____	**Я англичанин/англичанка** *Ya unglicharnin/unglicharnka*
I'm Scottish _____	**Я шотландец/шотландка** *Ya shutlarndyits/shutlarntka*
I'm Welsh _____	**Я валлиец/валлийка** *Ya vulleeyits/vulleeka*
I'm Irish _____	**Я ирландец/ирландка** *Ya irlarndits/irlarntka*
Do you speak_____ English/French/German?	**Вы говорите по-английски/по-французски/по-немецки?** *Vy guvureetye puh-angleeski/puh-frantsooski/puh-nimyetski?*
Is there anyone who _____ speaks...?	**Кто-нибудь говорит по-...?** *Ktor-neeboot guvureet puh...?*
I beg your pardon? _____	**Что вы сказали?** *Shtor vy skuzarli?*
I (don't) understand _____	**Я (не) понимаю** *Ya (nyeh) punnimahyu*
Do you understand me? _	**Вы меня понимаете?** *Vy minya punnimahyetyeh?*
Could you repeat that, ___ please?	**Повторите, пожалуйста** *Pufturreetyeh, puzharlooysta*
Could you speak more___ slowly, please?	**Говорите медленнее, пожалуйста** *Guvurreetyeh myaydlinyayeh, puzharlooysta*
What does that (word) ___ mean?	**Что это значит?/Что это слово означает?** *Shtor eto znarchit? Shtor eto slorva uzznuchahyet?*

| Is that similar to/the same as...? | Это (примерно) то же самое, как... ? |
| | *Eta (preemyairna) tor zheh sarmoyeh, kukk...?* |

| Could you write that down for me, please? | Напишите это для меня, пожалуйста |
| | *Nupisheetyeh eta dlya minya, puzharlooysta* |

| Could you spell that for me, please? | Скажите по буквам, пожалуйста |
| | *Skuzheetyeh pa bookvum, puzharlooysta* |

(See 1.8 Telephone alphabet)

| Could you point that out in this phrase book, please? | Покажите в этой книжке, пожалуйста |
| | *Pukkuzheetye vetoy kneeshkye, puzharlooysta* |

| One moment, please, I have to look it up | Минуточку, мне нужно поискать |
| | *Meenootuchkoo, mnyeh noozhna puh-eeskart* |

| I can't find the word/the sentence | Я не могу найти это слово/предложение |
| | *Ya nyeh muggoo nigh-tee eto slorva/ priddluzhayniyeh* |

| How do you say that in...? | Как это сказать по-...? |
| | *Kukk eta skuzzart puh...?* |

| How do you pronounce that? | Как это произносится? |
| | *Kukk eta pra-eeznorsitsa?* |

| May I introduce myself? | Разрешите представиться |
| | *Razrisheetyeh pridstarvitsa* |

3.2 Introductions

| My name's... | Меня зовут... |
| | *Minya zuvvoot...* |

| I'm... | Я... |
| | *Ya...* |

What's your name?	Как вас зовут?
	Kukk vas zuvvoot?
May I introduce...?	Можно вам представить?
	Morzhna varm pridstarvit?
This is my wife/ daughter/mother/ girlfriend	Это моя жена/дочь/мать/подруга
	Eto muyah zhinnah/dorch/mart/puddrooga
– my husband/son/ father/boyfriend	Это мой муж/сын/отец/друг
	Eto moy moozh/syn/uttyets/drook
How do you do	Здравствуйте, рад (рада) вас видеть
	Zdrarstvooytyeh, raht (rarda) vas veedit
Pleased to meet you	Очень приятно (познакомиться)
	Orchin priyartno (puznukormitsa)
Where are you from?	Откуда вы?
	Utkooda vy?
I'm from England/Scotland/Wales /Ireland	Я из Англии/Шотландии/ Уэльса/Ирландии
	Ya ees Arnglee-ee/Shutlarndee-ee/Oo-elsa/Eerlarndee-ee
What city do you live in?	В каком городе вы живёте?
	Fkukkorm gorudyeh vy zhyvyotyeh?
In..., it's near...	В...Это недалеко от...
	V...Eto nidullikor ut...
Have you been here long?	Вы уже давно здесь?
	Vy oozheh duvnor zdyess?
A few days	Несколько дней
	Nyeskulka dnyay
How long are you staying here?	Сколько вы здесь пробудете?
	Skorlka vy zdyess praboodyetyeh?
We're (probably) leaving tomorrow/in two weeks	Мы уезжаем (скорее всего) завтра/через две недели
	My ooyizhahyem (skorayeh vsivvor) zarftra/chayruss dvyeh nidyayli
Where are you staying?	Где вы остановились?
	Gdyeh vy ustunnuveelis?
In a hotel/an apartment	В гостинице/квартире
	Vgusteenitseh/kvarteeryeh

On a camp site _____	**В кемпинге**
	Fkempingeh
With friends/relatives ____	**У друзей/родственников**
	Oo droozyay/rortstvinneekuff
Are you here on your ____ own/with your family?	**Вы здесь один (одна)/с семьёй?**
	Vy zdyess udeen (udnah)/s simyoy?
I'm on my own_____	**я один (одна)**
	Ya udeen (udnah)
I'm with my_____ partner/wife/husband	**я с партнёром/женой/мужем**
	Ya spartnyorum/zhinoy/moozhum
– with my family _____	**я с семьёй**
	Ya s-simyoy
– with relatives_____	**я с родственниками**
	Ya srortstvinneekummi
– with a boy/girl_____ friend/friends	**я с другом/подругой/друзьями**
	Ya zdroogum/spuddroogoy/zdroozyarmi
Are you married?_____	**Вы женаты (замужем)?**
	Vy zhinarty (zarmoozhum)?
Do you have a steady ____ boyfriend/girlfriend?	**У тебя есть постоянный друг? (У тебя есть постоянная подруга?)**
	Oo tibyah yest pustuyahny drook? (Oo tibyah yest pustuyahnaya puddrooga?)
That's none of your_____ business	**Это вас не касается**
	Eto vas nyeh kasah-yitsa
I'm married_____	**Я женат (замужем)**
	Ya zhinart (zarmoozhum)
– single _____	**Я холостяк**
	Ya khullustyark
– separated _____	**Я живу отдельно**
	Ya zhivoo utdyelna
– divorced_____	**Я разведён (разведена)**
	Ya ruzvidyon (ruzvidyinah)
– a widow/widower_____	**Я вдова/вдовец**
	Ya vduvvah/vduvvyets
I live alone/with _____ someone	**Я живу один (одна)/я живу совместно**
	Ya zhivoo udeen (udnah)/Ya zhivoo suvvmyestna

Do you have any _____ children/grandchildren?	**У вас есть дети/внуки?**
	Oo vas yest dyayti/vnooki?
How old are you? _____	**Сколько вам лет?**
	Skorlka varm lyet?
How old is she/he? _____	**Сколько ей/ему лет?**
	Skorlka yey/yimoo lyet?
I'm... _____	**Мне...лет**
	Mnyeh...lyet
She's/he's... _____	**Ей/ему...лет**
	Yey/yimoo...lyet
What do you do for a ____ living?	**Кем вы работаете?**
	Kyem vy rubortayetyeh?
I work in an office _____	**Я работаю в учреждении**
	Ya rubortayu voochrizhdyaynii
I'm a student/ _____ I'm at school	**Я учусь/я учусь в школе**
	Ya oochoos/Ya oochoos vshkorlyeh
I'm unemployed _____	**Я безработный**
	Ya byizrubortny
I'm retired _____	**Я на пенсии**
	Ya nah pyensii
I'm on a disability _____ pension	**Я признан неспособным к работе**
	Ya preeznun nyespusorbnym krubortye
I'm a housewife _____	**я домохозяйка**
	Ya dummakhuzyayka
Do you like your job? ____	**Вам нравится ваша работа?**
	Varm nrarvitsa varsha rubborta?
Most of the time _____	**Иногда да, иногда нет**
	Eenugdah dah, eenugdah nyet
I usually do, but I prefer__ holidays	**В основном да, но отпуск мне нравится больше**
	Vusnuvnorm dah, noh ortpusk mnyeh nrarvitsa borlsheh

3.3 Starting/ending a conversation

Could I ask you _____ something?	**Можно вас спросить?** *Morzhna vas spruseet?*
Excuse me _____	**Извините/Простите** *Eezvineetyeh/Prusteetyeh*
Excuse me, could you ___ help me?	**Извините, вы не могли бы помочь?** *Eezvineetyeh, vy nyeh muglee by pumorch?*
Yes, what's the _____ problem?	**Да, что случилось?** *Dah, shtor sloocheeloss?*
What can I do for you? __	**Что я могу для вас сделать?** *Shtor ya muggoo dlya vas zdyelat?*
Sorry, I don't have time ___ now	**Простите, мне некогда** *Prusteetyeh, mnyeh nyekugda*
Do you have a light? ____	**Прикурить не найдётся?** *Prikureet nyeh nigh-dyotsa?*
May I join you? _____	**Можно сесть рядом с вами?** *Morzhna syest ryardum svarmi?*
Could you take a_____ picture of me/us? Press this button	**Вы не могли бы меня/нас сфотографировать? Нажмите эту кнопку** *Vy nyeh mugglee by minya sfuttugrufeeruvat? Nuzhmeetyeh etoo knorpkoo*
Leave me alone_____	**Оставь меня в покое** *Ustarf minya fpukoyeh*
Get lost _____	**Убирайся** *Oobirigh-sya*
Go away or I'll scream ___	**Если вы не отойдёте, я закричу** *Yesli vy nyeh uttuydyotyeh, ya zukrichoo*

3.4 Congratulations and condolences

Happy birthday/Happy___ name day	Поздравляю с днём рождения/Поздравляю с именинами
	Puzdruvlyayu zdnyom ruzhdyayniya/ Puzdruvlyayu seemineenummi
Please accept my _____ condolences	Мои соболезнования
	Ma-ee subbulyeznuvarniya
I'm very sorry for you ____	Я вам очень сочувствую
	Ya varm orchin suchoostvooyu

3.5 A chat about the weather

See also 1.5 The weather

It's so hot/cold today! ___	Как сегодня тепло/холодно!
	Kukk sivordnya tiplor/khorludna!
Nice weather, isn't it?____	Хорошая погода, не правда ли?
	Khurorshaya puggorda, nyeh prarvda lee?
What a wind/storm! _____	Какой ветер! Какая буря!
	Kukkoy vayter! Kukkaya boorya!
All that rain/snow! _____	Какой дождь/снег!
	Kukkoy dorzht/snyek!
All that fog!_____	Какой туман!
	Kukkoy toomarn!
Has the weather been ___ like this for long here?	Здесь уже давно такая погода?
	Zdyess oozheh duvnor tukkaya puggorda?
Is it always this hot/cold _ here?	Здесь всегда так тепло/холодно?
	Zdyess fsigdar tukk tiplor/khorludna?
Is it always this dry/wet __ here?	Здесь всегда так сухо/сыро?
	Zdyess fsigdar tukk sookha/syra?

3.6 Hobbies

Do you have any _____ **У вас есть хобби?**
hobbies? *Oo vas yest khorbi?*

I like knitting/ _____ **Я люблю**
reading/photography/ **вязать/читать/фотографировать/**
DIY **мастерить**
*Ya lyublyoo vyizart/chitart/
futugrufeeruvart/mustyereet*

I like music _____ **Я люблю музыку**
Ya lyublyoo moozyku

I like playing the _____ **Я люблю играть на гитаре/пианино**
guitar/piano *Ya lyublyoo eegrart nah geetaryeh/
pee-uneeno*

I like going to the _____ **Я люблю ходить в кино**
movies *Ya lyublyoo khudeet fkeenor*

I like travelling/ _____ **Я люблю путешествовать/заниматься**
sport/fishing/walking **спортом/ ловить рыбу/гулять**
*Ya lyublyoo pootyishestvuvart/zunimartsa
sportum/luveet ryboo/goolyart*

3.7 Being the host(ess)

See also 4 Eating out

Can I offer you a drink? __ **Разрешите предложить вам чего-нибудь**
выпить?
*Ruzrisheetyeh pridluzheet varm chivor-
niboot vypeet?*

What would you like _____ **Что ты будешь пить?**
to drink? *Shtor ty boodyesh peet?*

Something non-_____ **Что-нибудь без алкоголя, пожалуйста**
alcoholic, please *Shto-niboot byes ulkugorlya, puzharlooysta*

| Would you like a _____ cigarette/cigar/Russian papirorssa? | Вы хотите сигарету/сигару/папиросу? *Vy khuteetye sigaryetoo/sigaroo/ papirorssoo?* |
| I don't smoke_____ | Я не курю *Ya nyeh kooryoo* |

3.8 Invitations

Are you doing anything __ tonight?	Уы сегодня занят (занята)? *Ty sivordnya zarnyut (zanyutah)?*
Do you have any plans __ for today/this afternoon/tonight?	У вас есть планы на сегодня/сегодня днём/сегодня вечером? *Oo vas yest plarny nah sivordnya/sivordnya dnyom/sivordnya vaychiram?*
Would you like to go_____ out with me?	Хотите провести время со мной? *Khuteetyeh pruvistee vraymya sumnoy?*
Would you like to go_____ dancing with me?	Хотите со мной потанцевать? *Khuteetyeh sumnoy putantsivart?*
Would you like to have___ lunch/dinner with me?	Хотите вместе поужинать? *Khuteetyeh vmyestyeh pu-oozhinut?*
Would you like to come __ to the beach with me?	Хотите пойти со мной на пляж? *Khuteetyeh puytee sumnoy na plyahsh?*
Would you like to come __ into town with us?	Хотите пойти с нами в город? *Khuteetyeh puytee snarmi vgorut?*
Would you like to come __ and see some friends with us?	Хотите пойти с нами к друзьям? *Khuteetyeh puytee snarmi kdroozyarm?*
Shall we dance? _____	Потанцуем? *Putantsooyem?*
– sit at the bar? _____	Пойдём к бару? *Puydyom kbaroo?*
– get something to drink?	Выпьем что-нибудь? *Vypyum shto-niboot?*

– go for a walk/drive?	**Пойдём прогуляемся/покатаемся?**
	Puydyom prugoolyahyimsya/ pukutahyimsya?
Yes, all right	**Да, хорошо**
	Dah, khurushor
Good idea	**Неплохая идея**
	Nyiplukhaya eedyaya
No (thank you	**Нет (спасибо)**
	Nyet (spaseeba)
Maybe later	**Может быть, попозже**
	Morzhit byt, puporzha
I don't feel like it	**У меня нет настроения**
	Oo minya nyet nustruyayniya
I don't have time	**У меня нет времени**
	Oo minya nyet vraymini
I already have a date	**Я уже договорился (договорилась) с другим**
	Ya oozheh dugguvvureelsya (dugguvvureelas) zdroogeem
I'm not very good at dancing/volleyball/ swimming	**Я не умею танцевать/играть в волейбол/плавать**
	Ya nyeh oomyayu tantsivart/eegrart v vullayborl/plarvut

3.9 Paying a compliment

You look wonderful!	**Как вы хорошо выглядите!**
	Kukk vy khurushor vyglyadeetyeh!
I like your car!	**Красивая машина!**
	Kruseevaya musheena!
I like your ski outfit!	**Замечательный лыжный костюм!**
	Zamichartyelny lyzhny kustyoom!
You're a nice boy/girl	**Ты милый мальчик/Ты милая девочка**
	Ty meely marlchik/Ty meelaya dyevuchka

What a sweet child! _____	**Какой милый ребёнок!**
	Kukkoy meely ribyonuk!
You're a wonderful _____ dancer!	**Вы очень хорошо танцуете**
	Vy orchin khurushor tantsooyetyeh
You're a wonderful _____ cook!	**Вы очень хорошо готовите**
	Vy orchin khurushor gutorvityeh
You're a terrific soccer ___ player!	**Вы очень хорошо играете в футбол**
	Vy orchin khurushor eegrahyetyeh v futborl

3.10 Chatting someone up

I like being with you _____	**Мне с тобой очень приятно**
	Mnyeh stuboy orchin priyartno
I've missed you so much_	**Я так по тебе скучал (скучала)**
	Ya tak puh tibyeh skoocharl (skoocharla)
I dreamt about you _____	**Ты мне снился (снилась)**
	Ty mnyeh sneelsya (sneelas)
I think about you all day _	**Я целый день о тебе думаю**
	Ya tsely dyen o tibyeh doomuyu
You have such a sweet __ smile	**Ты так мило смеёшься**
	Ty tukk meelo smeeyoshsya
You have such beautiful__ eyes	**У тебя такие красивые глаза**
	Oo tibya tukkeeya kruseevy-yeh gluzzah
I'm in love with you_____	**Я в тебя влюблён (влюблена)**
	Ya ftibya vlyublyon (vlyublinah)
I'm in love with you too __	**Я в тебя тоже**
	Ya ftibya torzheh
I love you _____	**Я тебя люблю**
	Ya tibya lyublyoo
I love you too_____	**Я тебя тоже**
	Ya tibya torzheh
I don't feel as strongly ___ about you	**У меня не такие сильные чувства к тебе**
	Oo minya nyeh tukkeeyeh seelny-yeh choostva ktibyeh

I already have a _____ boyfriend/girlfriend	**У меня уже есть друг/подруга** *Oo minya oozheh yest drook/puddrooga*
I'm not ready for that ____	**Я ещё к этому не готов (готова)** *Ya yishchor ketummoo nyeh gutorf (gutorva)*
This is going too fast for me	**Всё происходит слишком быстро** *Fsyor pru-eeskhordit sleeshkum bystra*
Take your hands off me __	**Отстань** *Utstan*
Okay, no problem _____	**Ладно, ничего** *Lardna, nichivvor*
Will you stay with me ____ tonight?	**Ты останешься у меня сегодня на ночь?** *Ty ustarnyeshsya oo minya sivordnya narnuch?*
I'd like to go to bed ____ with you	**Я хочу с тобой спать** *Ya khuchoo stuboy spart*
Only if we use a condom_	**Только с презервативом** *Torlko sprezairvateevum*
We have to be careful about AIDS	**Мы должны быть осторожны из-за СПИДа** *My dulzhny byt usturorzhny eez-zah speeda*
That's what they all say __	**Все так говорят** *Vsyeh tukk guvuryat*
We shouldn't take any ____ risks	**Не будем рисковать** *Nyeh boodyem reeskuvart*
Do you have a condom? _	**У тебя есть презерватив?** *Oo tibya yest prezairvateef?*
No? In that case we _____ won't do it	**Нет? Тогда не будем** *Nyet? Tudgah nyeh boodyum*

45

3.11 Arrangements

When will I see _____ you again?	**Когда я тебя снова увижу?** *Kugdah ya tibya snorvah ooveezhu?*
Are you free over the ____ weekend?	**У вас есть время в выходные?** *Oo vas yest vraymya v vykhudny-yeh?*
What shall we arrange? __	**Как мы договоримся?** *Kukk my dugguvvureemsya?*
Where shall we meet? ___	**Где мы встретимся?** *Gdyeh my fstraytimsya?*
Will you pick me/us up? _	**Вы за мной/нами заедете?** *Vy za mnoy/narmi zayaydyetyeh?*
Shall I pick you up? _____	**Давайте я за вами заеду** *Duv-igh-tyeh ya za varmi zayaydu*
I have to be home by... __	**Я должен (должна) быть дома в...часов** *Ya dorlzhen (dulzhnah) byt dorma v... chussorf*
I don't want to see _____ you anymore	**Я вас больше не хочу видеть** *Ya vas borlshe nyeh khuchoo veedyet*
Can I take you home? ___	**Могу ли я отвезти вас домой?** *Muggoo lee ya utvistee vas dumoy?*

3.12 Saying goodbye

Can I write/call you?_____	**Я вам могу написать/позвонить?** *Ya vam muggoo napisart/puzvuneet?*
Will you write/call me? ___	**Вы мне напишете/позвоните?** *Vy mnyeh napeeshutyeh/puzvuneetyeh?*
Can I have your _____ address/phone number?	**Можно ваш адрес/телефон?** *Morzhno varsh ardris/tyeleforn?*
Thanks for everything_____	**Спасибо за всё** *Spaseeba za fsyoh*
It was very nice _____	**Было замечательно** *Byla zamichartelna*

Say hello to... _____	**Передай привет...**
	Pirid-igh preevyet...
All the best _____	**Всего самого лучшего**
	Fsivor sarmuva loochshiva
Good luck _____	**Дальнейших успехов**
	Dalnyayshikh oospyekhoff
When will you be back? _	**Когда ты снова придёшь?**
	Kugdah ty snorva preedyosh?
I'll be waiting for you _____	**Я буду тебя ждать**
	Ya boodoo tibya zhdart
I'd like to see you again_	**Я бы хотел (хотела) увидеть тебя ещё раз**
	Ya by khutyel (khutyela) ooveedit tibya yishchor rarss
I hope we meet _____ again soon	**Надеюсь, что мы скоро друг друга снова увидим**
	Nudyayus, shtor my skora drook drooga ooveedim
This is our address, _____ if you're ever in the UK	**Вот наш адрес, если вы когда-нибудь будете в Великобритании/Англии...**
	Vort narsh ardris, yesli vy kugdah-niboot boodyutyeh v Veleekobritarnii/Arnglii...
You'd be more than _____ welcome	**Будем рады вас видеть**
	Boodyem rardy vas veedit

4

Eating out

4.1 On arrival 49

4.2 Ordering 51

4.3 The bill 55

4.4 Complaints 55

4.5 Paying a compliment 57

4.6 The menu 57

4.7 Alphabetical list of drinks and dishes 58

● **In Russia** hotel restaurants usually provide three meals. Breakfast (завтрак, *zarftrak*) is between 8.00am and 10.00am and may offer juice, yoghurt, omelette, bread, butter, sausage or other meats, cheese, jam, cereal, tea and coffee. Lunch (обед, *ubyet*) is the main meal and is served between 12.00 and 1.30pm. It has at least three courses. The first is закуски, *zakooski* (starters, appetizers), which might be an egg dish, sliced meat or sausage, pickled cucumbers, fish, mushrooms, salads, brawn, or caviar. The soups often served after the *zakooski* can be a meal in themselves. The main course is meat, fish or game with some potatoes and vegetables (the latter are not as important as in British cooking). The sweet course might be pancakes, stewed fruit, a tart, or ice cream. The evening meal (ужин, *oozhin*) is from 7.00pm to 10.00pm. It is generally a lighter version of *ubyet* and may be no more than various kinds of open sandwiches with tea and coffee.

4.1 On arrival

I'd like to book a table for seven o'clock, please	**Можно заказать стол на семь часов?** *Morzhna zukkuzzart storl nah syem chassorf?*
I'd like a table for two, please	**Пожалуйста, столик на двоих** *Puzharlooysta, storlik nah dvu-eekh*
We've/we haven't booked	**Мы (не) заказывали** *My (nyeh) zukkarzyvarli*
Is the restaurant open yet?	**Кухня уже открыта?** *Kookhnya oozheh utkryta?*
What time does the restaurant open/close?	**Когда кухня открывается/закрывается?** *Kugdar kookhnya utkryvayetsya/zukkryvayetsya?*
Can we wait for a table?	**Мы можем подождать столик?** *My morzhum pudduzhdart storlik?*
Do we have to wait long?	**Нам придётся долго ждать?** *Narm preedyotsya dorlga zhdart?*

Вы заказывали?	Do you have a reservation?
На какую фамилию?	What name, please?
Сюда, пожалуйста	This way, please
Этот стол заказан	This table is reserved
Через пятнадцать минут столик освободится	We'll have a table free in fifteen minutes
Вы не могли бы подождать у бара?	Would you like to wait (at the bar)?

Is this seat taken? _____	**Это место свободно?**
	Eta myesta svubbordna?
Could we sit here/there? _	**Можно здесь/там сесть?**
	Morzhna zdyess/tarm syest?
Can we sit by the _____ window?	**Можно сесть у окна?**
	Morzhna syest oo ukknar?
Can we eat outside? _____	**Можно есть во дворе/на воздухе?**
	Morzhna yest vudvurryeh/nah vorzdookhyeh?
Do you have another _____ chair for us?	**Принесите нам ещё один стул, пожалуйста**
	Preenisseetyeh nahm yishchor udeen stool, puzharlooysta
Do you have a highchair?	**Принесите нам ещё детский стул, пожалуйста**
	Preenisseetyeh nahm yishchor dyetski stool, puzharlooysta
Is there a socket for _____ this bottle-warmer?	**Есть ли для этого нагревателя бутылочки розетка?**
	Yest lee dlya etuvva nuggrivartyelya bootyluchki ruzzyetka?
Could you warm up _____ this bottle/jar for me?	**Вы можете разогреть для меня эту бутылочку/баночку?**
	Vy morzhityeh ruzzugryayt dlya minya etoo bootyluchkoo/ barnuchkoo?

Not too hot, please_____	**Не очень горячо, пожалуйста**
	Nyeh orchin guryachor, puzharlooysta
Is there somewhere I ____ can change the baby's nappy?	**У вас есть помещение, где я могу переодеть ребёнка?**
	Oo vas yest pummishchayneeyeh, gdyeh ya muggoo pirreeuddyayt ribbyonka?
Where are the toilets? ___	**Где туалет?**
	Gdyeh too-ullyet?

4.2 Ordering

Waiter!_____	**Официант!**
	Uffitsiant!
Madam!_____	**Госпожа!**
	Guspuzhar!
Sir! _____	**Господин!**
	Guspuddeen!
We'd like something to __ eat/a drink	**Мы хотели бы поесть/попить**
	My khuttyayli by puyest/puppeet
Could I have a quick ____ meal?	**Могу я быстро поесть?**
	Muggoo ya bystra puyest?
We don't have much time	**У нас мало времени**
	Oo nuss marla vrayminee
We'd like to have a_____ drink first	**Мы сначала хотели бы чего-нибудь попить**
	My snucharla khuttyayli by chivvor-niboot puppeet
Could we see the _____ menu/wine list, please?	**Принесите нам меню/меню спиртных напитков, пожалуйста**
	Preenisseetyeh nahm minyoo/minyoo spirtnykh nuppeetkuff, puzharlooysta
Do you have a menu ____ in English?	**У вас есть меню на английском?**
	Oo vas yest minyoo na angleeskum?

Do you have a dish_____ of the day?/Tourist menu?	**У вас есть суточное меню?/У вас есть туристское меню?**
	Oo vas yest sootuchnoyeh minyoo?/Oo vas yest tooreestskoyeh minyoo?
We haven't made a_____ choice yet	**Мы ещё не выбрали**
	My yishchor nyeh vybrulli
What do you _____ recommend?	**Что бы вы порекомендовали?**
	***Shtor** by vy purrekumminduvvarli?*
What are the specialities _ of the region/the house?	**Какие фирменные блюда этой области/этого ресторана?**
	Kukkeeyeh feermyenny-yeh blyooda etoy orblasti/etuvva resturrarna?
I like strawberries/olives _	**Я люблю клубнику/оливки**
	Ya lyublyoo kloobneekoo/ulleefki
I don't like fish/meat... ____	**Я не люблю рыбу/мясо/ ...**
	Ya nyeh lyublyoo ryboo/myarsa
What's this? _____	**Что это?**
	Shtor eta?
Does it have...in it?_____	**Сюда входят...?**
	Syudar vkhordyut...?
Is this a hot or a _____ cold dish?	**Это горячее или холодное блюдо?**
	Eto guryarchiyeh eeli khullordnuyeh blyooda?
Is this sweet?_____	**Это сладкое блюдо?**
	Eto slartkoyeh blyooda?

Вы хотите поесть?	Would you like a drink first?
	Have you decided?
Вы выбрали?	What would you like to eat?
Что вы хотите пить?	Enjoy your meal.
	Would you like your steak rare,
Приятного аппетита.	medium or well done?
Вы хотите десерт/кофе/чай?	Would you like a dessert/coffee?

Is this spicy? _____	Это пикантное/острое блюдо?
	Eto peekarntnuyeh/orstruyeh blyooda?
Do you have anything ___ else, please?	У вас нет ничего другого?
	Oo vas nyet nichivvor droogorva?
I'm on a salt-free diet_____	Мне нельзя солёного
	Mnyeh nilzyah sullyonuvva
I can't eat pork _____	Мне нельзя свинины
	Mnyeh nilzyah sveeneeny
– sugar _____	Мне нельзя сладкого
	Mnyeh nilzyah slartkuvva
– fatty foods_____	Мне нельзя жирного
	Mnyeh nilzyah zheernuvva
– (hot) spices _____	Мне нельзя острого
	Mnyeh nilzyah orstruvva
I'm not allowed alcohol __	Мне нельзя пить
	Mnyeh nilzyah peet
I'll/we'll have what those _ people are having	То же, что и те люди заказали, пожалуйста
	Tor zheh, shtor ee tyeh lyoodyi zukkuzzarli, puzharlooysta
I'd like... _____	Я бы хотел (хотела)...
	Ya by knuttyel (khuttyela)...
We're not having a _____ starter	Закуска нам не нужна
	Zukkooska num nyeh noozhnah
The child will share _____ what we're having	Ребёнок поест что-нибудь из наших тарелок
	Ribyonuk pu-yest shtor-niboot eess narshikh taryelukk
Could I have some _____ more bread, please?	Ещё хлеба, пожалуйста
	Yishchor khlyeba, puzharlooysta
– a bottle of water/wine/ _ vodka please?	Ещё бутылку воды/вина/водки, пожалуйста
	Yishchor bootylku vuddy/veenah/vortki, puzharlooysta
– another helping of... ___	Ещё порцию...
	Yishchor portseeyu...

– some salt and pepper__	**Принесите, пожалуйста, соль и перец** *Prinisseetyeh, puzharlooysta, sorl ee pyayrits*
– a napkin_____	**Принесите, пожалуйста, салфетку** *Prinisseetyeh, puzharlooysta, sulfyetkoo*
– a spoon _____	**Принесите, пожалуйста, ложечку** *Prinisseetyeh, puzharlooysta, lorzhuchkoo*
– an ashtray _____	**Принесите, пожалуйста, пепельницу** *Prinisseetyeh, puzharlooysta, paypyelnitsoo*
– some matches _____	**Принесите, пожалуйста, спички** *Prinisseetyeh, puzharlooysta, speechki*
– some toothpicks _____	**Принесите, пожалуйста, зубочистки** *Prinisseetyeh, puzharlooysta, zoobucheestki*
– a glass of water _____	**Принесите, пожалуйста, стакан воды** *Prinisseetyeh, puzharlooysta, stukkarn vuddy*
– a straw (for the child) __	**Принесите, пожалуйста, соломинку (для ребёнка)** *Prinisseetyeh, puzharlooysta, sulormeenku (dlyah ribyonka)*
Enjoy your meal! _____	**Приятного аппетита!** *Preeyartnuvva appeteeta!*
You too!_____	**Того же** *Tuvvor zhe*
Cheers! _____	**(За) ваше здоровье!** *(Zah) varsha zdurorvyeh!*
The next round's _____ on me	**В следующий раз я плачу** *Fslyedooyushchee rass ya pluchoo*

4.3 The bill

See also 8.2 Settling the bill

How much is this dish? __	**Сколько стоит это блюдо?**
	Skorlka stor-eet eto blyooda?
Could I have the bill, ____ please?	**Счёт, пожалуйста**
	Shchot, puzharlooysta
All together_____	**Всё вместе**
	Fsyo vmyestyeh
Everyone pays separately	**Каждый платит за себя**
	Karzhdy plartit za sibya
Could we have the menu again, please?	**Можно ещё раз посмотреть меню?**
	Morzhna yishchor rass pusmutrayt minyoo?
The...is not on the bill____	**...не занесено в счёт**
	...nyeh zunnissinor fshchot

4.4 Complaints

It's taking a very _____ long time	**Это очень долго длится**
	Eto orchin dorlga dleetsya
We've been here an ____ hour already	**Мы сидим здесь уже час**
	My sideem zdyess oozheh charss
This must be a mistake __	**Это, должно быть, ошибка**
	Eto, dulzhnor byt, ushypka
This is not what I_____ ordered	**Это не то, что я заказывал (заказывала)**
	Eto nyeh tor, shto ya zukkarzyval (zukkarzyvala)
I ordered... _____	**Я попросил (попросила)...**
	Ya pupprusseel (pupprusseela)...
There's a dish missing ___	**Одного блюда не хватает**
	Udnuvvor blyooda nyeh khvutigh-yet
This is broken/not clean _	**Это сломано/грязно**
	Eto slormunna/gryahzna

The food's cold _____	**Еда холодная**
	Yiddah khulordnaya
– not fresh _____	**Еда несвежая**
	Yiddah nisvayzhaya
– too salty/sweet/spicy __	**Еда слишком солёная/сладкая/острая**
	Yiddah sleeshkum sulyonaya/
	slartkaya/orstraya
The meat's not done _____	**Мясо не прожарилось**
	Myarsa nyeh pruzhareeluss
– overdone _____	**Мясо пережарено**
	Myarsa pirreezharina
– tough _____	**Мясо жёсткое**
	Myarsa zhostkaya
– off _____	**Мясо несвежее**
	Myarsa nisvayzhaya
Could I have something __ else instead of this?	**Дайте мне вместо этого что-нибудь другое, пожалуйста**
	Digh-tye mnyeh vmyesta etuvva shtor-niboot droogor-yeh, puzharlooysta
The bill/this amount is ___ not right	**По-моему, здесь неправильно**
	Puh-moyemoo zdyess nyeprarveelna
We didn't have this _____	**У нас этого не было**
	Oo nuss etuvva nyeh bylo
There's no paper in the __ toilet	**В туалете нет бумаги**
	Ftooalyetyeh nyet boomargi
Do you have a _____ complaints book?	**У вас есть книга жалоб?**
	Oo vuss yest kneega zharlupp?
Will you call the _____ manager, please?	**Позовите, пожалуйста, начальника**
	Puzzuveetyeh, puzharlooysta, nacharlnika

4.5 Paying a compliment

That was a wonderful____ **Мы прекрасно поели**
meal *My prikrarsna pu-yayli*

The food was excellent ___ **Всё было очень вкусно**
Fsyo byla orchin fkoosna

The...in particular was ___ **Особенно...был исключительным**
delicious *Usorbinna...byl eesklyucheetyelnym*

4.6 The menu

безалкогольные напитки
non-alcoholic drinks

вина
wines

вторые блюда
main course

горячие супы
hot soups

десерт
dessert

дичь
game

закуски
starters

завтрак
breakfast

кофе
coffee

мясо
meat

национальные блюда
national dishes

обед
lunch

овощи
vegetables

первые блюда
first courses

птица
poultry

салаты
salads

соки
juices

спиртные/алкоголь ные напитки
spirits/alcoholic drinks

супы
soups

ужин
dinner/evening meal

фирменные блюда
specialities of the house

фрукты
fruit

холодные супы
cold soups

чай
tea

абрикос apricot
ананас pineapple
антрекот rib steak
апельсин, апельсиновый orange
арбуз water-melon
ассорти мясное/рыбное meat platter/fish platter
баклажаны, из баклажанов aubergines
банан banana
баранина, из баранины mutton
бефстроганов beef stroganov
бифштекс rumpsteak
блины/блинчики pancakes
бобы beans
борщ borshch (beetroot soup)
бренди brandy

брынза ewe's milk cheese
буженина boiled pork
булочка bread roll
бульон clear soup
бутерброд open sandwich
вальдшнеп woodcock
вареники dumplings
варёный (-ая, -ое) cooked
варенье, с вареньем preserves, with preserves
ватрушка curd cheese bun
вермишель vermicelli
вермут vermouth
ветчина, с ветчиной raw ham, with ham
вино (белое, красное, сухое, сладкое) wine (white, red, dry, sweet)

виноград grapes
виски (со льдом) whisky (on the rocks)
вишни, вишнёвый cherries, cherry (adj.)
вырезка fillet
гарнир, с гарниром garnish, with trimmings
говядина beef
горох, гороховый peas, from peas
горчица mustard
гранат, гранатовый pomegranate, from pomegranate
грейпфрут, грейпфрутовый grapefruit, from grapefruit
грибной (-ое, -ая)/из грибов from mushrooms/fungi
грибы, с грибами mushrooms/fungi
груша pear

58

гуляш
goulash

гусь
goose

джем jam

джин (с тоником)
gin (and tonic)

дыня
honeydew melon

ёрш
ruff (freshwater fish)/
  mixture of vodka and
  beer (or wine)

жареный (-ая, -ое)
roasted/fried/grilled/br
  oiled

желе
jelly/aspic

жюльен
stew

заливной (-ая, -ое)
jellied/in aspic

заяц
hare

изюм
raisins

икра (красная,
чёрная)
caviar (red, black)

индейка
turkey

кабачки
courgettes

камбала
plaice

капуста, с капустой
cabbage, with
  cabbage

капуста (кислая,
  красная, цветная)
cabbage (sauerkraut,
  red cabbage,
  cauliflower)

карась, карп
carp

картофель
potatoes

каша
buckwheat

квас
kvass

кефир
buttermilk

кильки
sprats

клубника
strawberries

клюква,
  клюквенный
cranberry, from
  cranberries

колбаса
sausage

компот
stewed fruit

коньяк cognac

копчёный
smoked

котлеты
Russian meatballs

котлеты по-киевски
chicken kiev

кофе (чёрный)
coffee (black)

краб, из крабов
crab, from crab

креветки
prawns

кролик
rabbit

кукуруза
maize

курица, с курицей
chicken, with
  chicken

куриный, из кур
from chicken

куропатка
partridge

лангет
roast sirloin

лапша
noodles/noodle
  soup

лещ bream

ликёр
liqueur

лимон, с лимоном
lemon, with lemon

лимонад
lemonade

лососина/лосось
salmon

лук, с луком
onion, with onion

майонез, под
майонезом
mayonnaise

макароны
macaroni

макрель
mackerel

мандарин,
мандариновый
mandarin orange, from
mandarins

маринованный (-ая,
-ое)
pickled

маслины
black olives

мясо, мясной
meat, from meat

начинка, с начинкой
filling/with filling

овощи, овощной (-ая, -ое)
vegetables, vegetable
(adj.)

огурец, из огурцов
ridge cucumber, made
from ridge
cucumbers

окорок
boiled ham

окрошка
cold soup with kvass,
meat and vegetables

окунь perch

оладьи
fritters

оливки
green olives

орехи
nuts

осётр/осетрина
sturgeon

отбивная
котлета
chop

отварной (-ая, ое)
boiled/poached

палтус
halibut

паровой (-ая, ое)
steamed

паштет
pâté

пельмени
dumplings filled with
meat

перепел
quail

петрушка
parsley

печёнка
liver

печёный (-ая, ое)
baked

печенье
a cake/biscuit

пиво beer

пирог/пирожок
pie

пирожное
pastries

пити
mutton soup

плов
pilaff

поджарка
grilled meat

помидоры, из
помидоров
tomatoes, from
tomatoes

пончик
deep-fried little pie

порей
leek

поросёнок/
поросята
sucking pig

портвейн
port

похлёбка
thin soup

почки
kidneys

простокваша
yoghurt

пряник
spice cake

пудинг
pudding

пунш
punch

пюре
purée

рагу
ragout

рак
crayfish

рассольник
soup with pickled cucumbers

расстегай
small fish pie

редис(ка), из редиски
radish, from radishes

репа
turnip

рис, рисовый
rice

ром
rum

ростбиф
roast beef

рыбный (-ая, ое)
fish

рябчик
hazel grouse

ряженка
yoghurt made with evaporated milk

салат
salad

сардины
sardines

сахар, без сахара, с сахаром
sugar, without sugar, with sugar

свёкла
beetroot

свекольник
iced beetroot soup

свинина, из свинины
port

селёдка/сельдь
herring

сёмга
salmon

слива/со сливами
plum/with plums

сливовый
plum (adj.)

сливки (взбитые), со сливками
cream (whipped), with cream

сметана, со сметаной, в сметане
sour cream, with sour cream, in sour cream

смородина
currants

солёный (-ая, ое)
salted

солонина
salted beef

соль
salt

сом
catfish

сосиски/сардельки
frankfurter sausages/bangers

соус, под белым соусом
sauce, in white sauce

спаржа, спаржевый
asparagus

студень
fish in aspic/brawn

судак
zander

суп
soup

сыр
cheese

сырники
curd cheese fritters

сырок
curds pressed into a cheese shape

творог, с творогом
cottage cheese, with cottage cheese

телятина
veal

тефтели
meatballs

топлёное молоко
evaporated milk

торт
large many-layered cake

треска cod

тресковая печень
cod-liver

тунец
tuna

тушёный (-ая, ое)
braised

тыква
pumpkin

угорь eel

уксус
vinegar

устрицы
oysters

утка duck

уха
fish soup

фаршированный (-ая, ое)
stuffed

фасоль
beans

филе
fillet

финики
dates

форель
trout

фрукты, фруктовый
fruit

харчо
mutton soup with rice

херес
sherry

хлеб (белый, чёрный)
bread (white, black)

хрен, с хреном
horseradish, with horseradish

цыплёнок/цыплята
pullet/pullets

цыплёнок табака
Georgian boned chicken

чай tea

чахохбили из кур
Caucasian chicken meatballs

чебуреки
Caucasian deep-fried stuffed dumplings

черемша
Caucasian wild onion

черешня
cherries

черника
bilberry

чеснок, с чесноком
garlic, with garlic

шампанское (сухое, полусладкое, сладкое)
champagne (dry, demi-sec, sweet)

шашлык
shishkebab

шницель
schnitzel

шоколад, шоколадный
chocolate

шпинат
spinach

шпроты
sprats

щи
cabbage soup

щи кислые
sauerkraut soup

щи зелёные с яйцом
sorrel soup with beaten egg

эскалоп
cutlet

яблоко, с яблоками
apple, with apples

яблоко в тесте
apple pie

яблочный
apple (adj.)

язык
tongue

яйцо (всмятку, вкрутую)
egg (soft-boiled, hard-boiled)

яичница
fried egg

5.1 Asking for directions 64

5.2 Customs 65

5.3 Luggage 68

5.4 Traffic signs 69

5.5 The car 70

The parts of a car 72

5.6 The petrol station 70

5.7 Breakdown and repairs 74

5.8 The bicycle/moped 76

The parts of a bicycle 78

5.9 Renting a vehicle 77

5.10 Hitchhiking 80

5.1 Asking for directions

Excuse me, could I ask __ you something?	**Извините, можно вас спросить?** *Eezvineetyeh, morzhna vuss sprusseet?*
I've lost my way _____	**Я заблудился (заблудилась)** *Ya zubloodeelsya (zubloodeelas)*
Is there a(n)... _____ around here?	**Вы не знаете, здесь поблизости...?** *Vy nyeh znah-yetyeh, zdyess publeezusti...?*
Is this the way to...? _____	**Это дорога в...?** *Eto durrorga v...?*
Could you tell me _____ how to get to the... (name of place)by car/on foot?	**Вы не подскажете, как доехать/ дойти до...?** *Vy nyeh pudskarzhityeh, kukk duh-yekhat/duytee dor...?*
What's the quickest _____ way to...?	**Как можно быстрее доехать до...?** *Kukk morzhna bystrayeh duh-yekhat dor...?*
How many kilometres____ is it to...?	**Сколько километров до...?** *Skorlka keelumyetruff dor...?*
Could you point it _____ out on the map?	**Покажите на карте, пожалуйста** *Pukkuzheetyeh nah kartyeh, puzharlooysta*

Я не знаю, я не отсюда	I don't know, I don't know my way around here
Вы едете в неправильном направлении	You're going the wrong way
Вам нужно вернуться в...	You have to go back to...
Вы увидите, там будет написано	From there on just follow the signs
Там вам придётся снова спросить	When you get there, ask again

прямо	улица	река
straight ahead	the street	the river
налево	светофор	путепровод
left	the traffic lights	the flyover
направо	туннель	мост
right	the tunnel	the bridge
повернуть	знак "уступите дорогу"	железнодорожный переезд/шлагбаум
turn	the 'give way' sign	level crossing/ barrier
последовать	здание	указатель направления...
follow	the building	the sign pointing to...
перейти cross	на углу at the corner	стрелка the arrow
перекрёсток		
the intersection		

5.2 Customs

● **Tourists wishing** to visit the Russian Federation must have a passport that is valid for the entire period that they will be in the country, and they must have a visa that is also valid for the specific period of their stay. Visas for visits that are arranged by tour companies are usually obtained by the company. Children who are included in the passport of one of the parents are added to the visa of that parent.

Visa application forms can be obtained from the Consulate General of the Russian Federation in London, 5 Kensington Palace Gardens, London W8 4QS, tel. 0207 4957570, or the Consulate General in Edinburgh, 58 Melville Street, Edinburgh EG3 7HL, tel. 0131 225 7098. If you are going to Russia for a period of more than 3 months you must present a valid AIDS certificate.

At the border you must sign a customs declaration in which you state how much money you are carrying. A similar declaration is to be signed when you leave the country, There is no limit to the amount of foreign money and travellers' cheques you can take into Russia, but Russian money cannot be imported or exported and works of art/antiques may not be taken out without a licence.

Ваш паспорт, пожалуйста	Your passport, please
Ваша декларация, пожалуйста	Your green card, please
Технический паспорт, пожалуйста	Your vehicle documents, please
Ваша виза, пожалуйста	Your visa, please
Куда вы едете?	Where are you heading?
Сколько вы собираетесь пробыть?	How long are you planning to stay?
Есть ли у вас что-нибудь, подлежащее оплате пошлиной?	Do you have anything to declare?
Откройте это, пожалуйста	Open this, please

My children are entered on this passport	Мои дети вписаны в этот паспорт *Ma-ee dyayti fpeesunny vetut parsport*
I'm travelling through ____	Я проездом *Ya pru-yezdum*
I'm going on holiday to...___	Я еду в отпуск в... *Ya yay-doo vortpoosk v...*
I'm on a business trip____	У меня деловая поездка *Oo minya dyeluvvaya pu-yestka*
I don't know how long ____ I'll be staying yet	Я ещё не знаю, сколько я пробуду *Ya yishchor nyeh znah-yu, skorlka ya pruboodoo*
I'll be staying here for____ a weekend	Я на выходные *Ya nah vykhudny-yeh*
– for a few days_____	Я на несколько дней *Ya nah nyeskulka dnyay*

– for a week _____	Я на неделю
	Ya nah nidyaylyu
–for two weeks _____	Я на две недели
	Ya nah dvyeh nidyayli
I've got nothing to_____ declare	У меня нет ничего, что подлежит оплате пошлиной
	Oo minya nyet nichivvor, shto pudlizhyt uplartye porshlinoy
I've got...with me _____	У меня с собой есть...
	Oo minya s suboy yest...
– ...cartons of cigarettes _	У меня с собой есть блок сигарет
	Oo minya s suboy yest blork seegurryet
– ...bottles of..._____	У меня с собой есть бутылки...
	Oo minya s suboy yest bootylki...
– some souvenirs _____	У меня с собой есть несколько сувениров
	Oo minya s suboy yest nyeskulka soovineeruff
These are personal _____ effects	Это личные вещи
	Eto leechny-yeh vyayshchi
These are not new _____	Эти вещи не новые
	Eti vyayshchi nyeh norvy-yeh
Here's the receipt _____	Вот чек
	Vort chyek
This is for private use_____	Это для меня
	Eto dlya minya
How much import duty __ do I have to pay?	Сколько нужно заплатить за ввоз?
	Skorlka noozhna zuplutteet za v-vorz?
Can I go now? _____	Можно пройти?
	Morzhno pruytee?

5.3 Luggage

Porter! _____	**Носильщик!**
	Nusseelshchik!
Could you take this_____ luggage to...?	**Отнесите багаж в...,пожалуйста**
	Utnisseeetyeh buggarsh v...,puzharlooysta
How much do I _____ owe you?	**Сколько с меня?**
	Skorlka s minya?
Where can I find a_____ luggage trolley?	**Где тележки для багажа?**
	Gdyeh tilyeshki dlya bugguzhar?
Could you store this _____ luggage for me?	**Могу я сдать багаж на хранение?**
	Muggoo ya zdart buggarsh na khrunyayniya?
Where are the luggage___ lockers?	**Где автоматическая камера хранения?**
	Gdyeh aftummuteecheskaya karmyera khrunyayniya?
I can't get the locker ____ open	**Сейф не открывается**
	Sayf nyeh unkryvahyetsya
How much is it per item _ per day?	**Сколько стоит сейф в день?**
	Skorlko stor-it sayf v dyen?
This is not my bag/_____ suitcase	**Это не моя сумка/Это не мой чемодан**
	Eto nyeh muyah soomka/Eto nyeh moy chimmuddarn
There's one item/bag/ ___ suitcase missing still	**Не хватает ещё одной вещи/сумки/не хватает ещё одного чемодана**
	Nyeh khvuttah-yet yishchor udnoy vyayshchi/soomki/nyeh khvuttah-yet yishchor udnuvvor chimmuddarna
My suitcase is damaged _	**Мой чемодан повреждён**
	Moy chimmuddarn puvrizhdyon

5.4 Traffic signs

Russia uses the international traffic signs, but there are two special forms:

means **STOP**   *means END OF RESTRICTION*

You may also come across the following notices when driving:

Берегитесь автомобиля!
Watch out for cars

велосипедисты
cyclists

внимание, впереди ведутся работы
road works ahead

(внимание) пешеходы
Watch out for pedestrians

встречное движение
oncoming traffic

въезд запрещён
no entry

ГАИ
traffic police

движение в один ряд
single-file traffic

держитесь правой стороны
keep to the right

камнепад
falling rocks

обгон запрещён
no overtaking

обочина
kerb

объезд
diversion

ограничение скорости
speed limit

одностороннее движение
one-way traffic

опасно dangerous

опасный поворот
dangerous bend

остановка автобуса
bus stop

остановка запрещена
no stopping

переход
crossing

плохая дорога
bad surface

светофор через сто метров
lights ahead 100 metres

стоп
stop

стоянка запрещена
no parking

сужение дороги
road narrows

такси
taxi

таможня
Customs

5.5 The car

● **It is compulsory** for tourists motoring in Russia to have a valid
international driving permit and carry first aid kit, fire extinguishers, a
warning triangle, and a headlamp/beam converter. (For up-to-the-
minute information contact the AA.) It is also recommended to take
with you at least spare fan-belts, bulbs and plugs.

Driving is on the right. Avoid night-driving. Seat-belts are
compulsory for the driver and front-seat passenger. Fines are usually
on the spot. The speed limit is 37 mph (60 km/h) in built-up areas, 55
mph (88 km/h) outside, and 43 mph (68 km/h) everywhere for
motorists with less than 2 years' driving experience except where a
lower limit is already indicated.

Personal safety. Before planning any visit to Russia at the moment it
is imperative to contact the Foreign and Commonwealth Office Travel
Advice Bureau.

5.6 The petrol station

● **Petrol in Russia** is often in short supply and filling stations few and
far between. It is advisable to take reserve petrol in a can (import
duty is payable on this). Petrol coupons can be bought with hard
currency at the border and foreign currency is preferred when buying
petrol. Unleaded petrol is not generally available. The most common
diesel fuel is Солярка (*Solyarka*).

How many kilometres to _
the next petrol station,
please?

**Сколько километров до следующей
заправочной станции?**
*Sko**rl**ka keelumm**ye**truff dussl**ay**dooyushchi
zupp**r**arvochnoy sta**rn**tsii?*

I would like...litres of..., please	**Мне нужно...литров**
	*Mnyeh no**o**zhna...l**ee**truff*
– petrol	**Мне нужно...литров бензина**
	*Mnyeh no**o**zhna ... l**ee**truff benz**ee**na*
– super	**Мне нужно...литров бензина высшего качества**
	*Mnyeh no**o**zhna...l**ee**truff benz**ee**na vyss-shiva k**ar**chistva*
– diesel	**Мне нужно...литров дизеля**
	*Mnyeh no**o**zhna...l**ee**truff d**ee**zilya*
I would like...roubles' worth of petrol, please	**Мне нужен бензин за...рублей**
	*Mnyeh no**o**zhun benz**ee**n zah...r**oo**blyay*
Fill her up, please	**Полный бак, пожалуйста**
	*P**or**lny bark, puzh**ar**looysta*
Could you check...?	**Проверьте, пожалуйста...**
	*Pruvy**air**tye, puzh**ar**looysta...*
– the oil level	**Проверьте, пожалуйста, уровень масла**
	*Pruvy**air**tye, puzh**ar**looysta, **oo**ruvvin m**ar**ssla*
– the tyre pressure	**Проверьте, пожалуйста, накачку шин**
	*Pruvy**air**tye, puzh**ar**looysta, nukk**ar**chkoo shin*
Could you change the oil, please?	**Поменяйте масло, пожалуйста**
	*Pumin**yigh**-tyeh m**ar**sslo, puzh**ar**looysta*
Could you clean the windows/the windscreen, please?	**Вымойте стёкла/ветровое стекло, пожалуйста**
	*V**y**moytyeh st**yo**kla/vitruv**o**yeh stikl**or**, puzh**ar**looysta*
Could you give the car a wash, please?	**Помойте машину, пожалуйста**
	*Pum**o**ytyeh mush**i**nu, puzh**ar**looysta*

The parts of a car

battery	аккумулятор	akkoomoolyartur
rear light	задняя фара	zardnyaya fara
rear-view mirror	зеркало заднего обзора	zyairkulla zardnyivo ubzora
reversing light	фара для ездызадним ходом	fara dlya yizdy zardnim khordum
aerial	антенна	untaynna
car radio	автомобильный радиоприёмник	ufftummubeelny radiopreeyomnik
petrol tank	бензобак	binzobark
sparking plugs	свечи зажигания	svyaychi zuzhigarniya
fuel filter/pump	топливный фильтр/насос	torplivny feeltr/nussors
wing mirror	наружное зеркало	nuroozhnoyeh zyairkulla
bumper	бампер	barmpyer
carburettor	карбюратор	karbyurartor
crankcase	масляный картер	marslyuny kartyer
cylinder	цилиндр	tsyleendr
ignition	контакты	kuntarkty
warning light	контрольная лампочка	kuntrorlnaya larmpuchka
dynamo	динамо	deenarmo
accelerator	педаль акселератора	pidarl ukselirartora
handbrake	ручной тормоз	roochnoy tormus
valve	клапан	klarpun
silencer	глушитель	gloosheetyel
headlight	фара	fara
crank shaft	коленчатый вал	kullyenchutty varl
air filter	воздушный фильтр	vuzdooshny feeltr
engine block	моторный блок	muttorny blork
camshaft	распределительный вал	ruspridyileetyelny varl

oil filter/pump	масляный фильтр/насос	marslyany feeltr/nussorss
dipstick	щуп для замера уровня масла	shchoop dlya zummyaira ooruvnya marsla
pedal	педаль	pidarl
door	дверь	dvyer
radiator	радиатор	ruddiartor
brake disc	тормозной диск	zuppussnor-yeh
spare wheel	запасное колесо	zuppussnor-yeh kullissor
indicator	указатель поворота	ookuzzartyel puvvurorta
windscreen wiper	дворник	dvornik
shock absorbers	амортизаторы	ummurtizartury
sunroof	раздвижная крыша	ruzzdvizhnahya krysha
spoiler	спойлер	spoylyer
starter motor	стартовый двигатель	startuvvy dveeguttyel
steering column	картер рулевого управления	karter roolyevorva oopruvlyayniya
exhaust pipe	выхлоп	vykhlup
seat belt	ремень безопасности	rimyen byezupparsnusti
fan	вентилятор	ventilyartor
distributor cables	провода свечи зажигания	pruvuddar svichee zuzhygarniya
gear lever	рычаг переключения передач	rychark pireeklyoochayniya pireedarch
windscreen	ветровое стекло	vitruvvoryeh styiklor
water pump	водяной насос	vuddyunnoy nussorss
wheel	колесо	kullissor
hubcap	колпак колеса	kulpark kullissar
piston	поршень	porshin

5.7 Breakdown and repairs

I'm having car trouble. Could you give me a hand?	**У меня авария. Вы можете мне помочь?** *Oo minya uvvariya. Vy morzhityeh mnyeh pummorch?*
I've run out of petrol	**У меня кончился бензин** *Oo minya korncheelsya binzeen*
I've locked the keys in the car	**Я оставил(а) ключи в машине** *Ya ustarveel(a) klyoochee vmushinyeh*
The car/motorbike/ moped won't start	**Машина/мотоцикл/мопед не заводится** *Mushina/muttertsykl/muppyet nyeh zuvvorditsa*
Could you call out a mechanic for me, please?	**Вызовите скорую техническую помощь, пожалуйста** *Vyzuvveetye skorooyu tyekhneechiskooyu pormushch, puzharlooysta*
Could you call a garage for me, please?	**Позвоните в гараж, пожалуйста** *Puzvunneetyeh vgurrarsh, puzharlooysta*
Could you give me a lift to...?	**Вы меня не подвезёте до...?** *Vy minya nyeh pudvizyotyeh duh...?*
– a garage/into town?	**Вы меня не подвезёте до гаража/города?** *Vy minya nyeh pudvizyotyeh duh gurruzhar/gorudda?*
– a phone booth?	**Вы меня не подвезёте до телефонной будки?** *Vy minya nyeh pudvizyotyeh duh tyelifornoy bootki?*
– an emergency phone?	**Вы меня не подвезёте до аварийного телефона?** *Vy minya nyeh pudvizyotyeh duh uvvurreenuvva tyeliforna?*
Can we take my bicycle/moped?	**Можно взять велосипед (мотоцикл) с собой?** *Morzhna vzyart vilosipyet (muttatsikl) s suboy?*

Could you tow me to a garage?	Вы можете отбуксировать меня до гаража?
	Vy morzhityeh utbookseeruvat minya duh gurruzhar?
There's probably something wrong with...(See page 72)	Скорее всего, что-то с ...
	Skurryayeh fsivor, shtor-to s ...
Can you fix it?	Вы можете это починить?
	Vy morzhityeh eto puchineet?
Could you fix my tyre?	Вы можете заклеить шину?
	Vy morzhityeh zukklayit shinoo?
Could you change this wheel?	Вы можете поменять колесо?
	Vy morzhityeh pumminyart kullissor?
Can you fix it so it'll get me to...?	Вы можете это так починить, чтобы я доехал(а) до ...?
	Vy morzhityeh eto tukk puchineet, shtorby ya duhyekhal(a) dor ...?
Which garage can help me?	В каком гараже мне могут помочь?
	Fkukkorm gurruzheh mnyeh morgoot pumorch?
When will my car/bicycle be ready?	Когда моя машина будет готова?/ огда мой велосипед будет готов?
	Kugdar muyah mushina boodyet guttorva?/Kugdar moy vilusipyet boodyet guttorff?
Can I wait for it here?	Вы сделаете это при мне?
	Vy zdyelayetyeh eta pree mnyeh?
How much will it cost?	Сколько это будет стоить?
	Skorlka eta boodyet stor-eet?
Could you itemise the bill?	Вы можете составить подробный счёт?
	Vy morzhityeh sustarveet puddrorbny shchot?
Can I have a receipt for the insurance?	Можно квитанцию для страховки?
	Morzhna kveetarntseeyu dlyah strakhorfki?

5.8 The bicycle/moped

● **Cycle paths** are rare in Russia and there is generally very little special provision on the roads for cycles/mopeds

У меня нет запчастей для вашей машины/вашего велосипеда	I don't have parts for your car/bicycle
Я должен забрать запчасти в другом месте	I have to get the parts from somewhere else
я должен заказать запчасти	I have to order the parts
Это займёт полдня	That'll take half a day
Это займёт день	That'll take a day
Это займёт несколько дней	That'll take a few days
Это займёт неделю	That'll take a week
Ваша машина окончательно сломана	Your car is a write-off
Ничего нельзя сделать	It can't be repaired
Машина/мотоцикл/мопед /велосипед будет готов(а) в...часов	The car/motor bike/moped/bicycle will be ready at...o'clock

5.9 Renting a vehicle

I'd like to rent a... _____	**Я бы хотел(а) взять напрокат ...**
	Ya by khuttyayl(a) vzyart nupprukkart
Do I need a (special) _____ licence for that?	**Для этого нужны специальные права?**
	Dlyah etuvva noozhny spetseearlny-yeh pruvvar?
I'd like to rent the...for... __	**Я хочу взять напрокат ... на ...**
	Ya khuchoo vzyart nuprukkart ... nah ...
– one day _____	**Я хочу взять напрокат ... на один день**
	Ya khuchoo vzyart nuprukkart ... nah uddeen dyen
– two days _____	**Я хочу взять напрокат ... на два дня**
	Ya khuchoo vzyart nuprukkart ... nah dvah dnyah
How much is that per ____ day/week?	**Сколько это стоит в день/в неделю?**
	Skorlka eto stor-yit v dyen/v nidyaylyu?
How much is the _____ deposit?	**Сколько составляет залог?**
	Skorlka sustuvlyahyet zullork?
Could I have a receipt ___ for the deposit?	**Можно квитанцию об уплате залога?**
	Morzhna kveetarntseeyou ub ooplartyeh zullorga?
How much is the _____ surcharge per kilometre?	**Какова доплата за километр?**
	Kukkuvvar dupplarta za keelomyetr?
Does that include _____ petrol?	**Это включая бензин?**
	Eto fklyuchahya benzeen?
Does that include _____ insurance?	**Это включая страховку?**
	Eto fklyuchahya strukhorfkoo?
What time can I pick _____ the...up tomorrow?	**Во сколько я могу забрать ... завтра?**
	Vuh skorlka ya muggoo zubbrart ... zarftra?
When does the...have ___ to be back?	**Когда мне вернуть ... ?**
	Kugdar mnyeh virnoot ...?
Where's the petrol tank? _	**Где бак?** *Gdyeh bark?*
What sort of fuel does ___ it take?	**Какое заливать горючее?**
	Kukkoryeh zulleevart gurryoochiyeh?

The parts of a bicycle

rear lamp	задний фонарь	*zardnee funnar*
rear wheel	заднее колесо	*zardnyeyeh kullissor*
(luggage) carrier	багажник	*buggarzhnik*
bicycle fork	распределительная головка	*russpridyeleetyelnaya gullorfka*
bell	звонок	*zvunnork*
inner tube	камера шины	*karmera shiny*
tyre	покрышка шины	*pukkryshka shiny*
crank	кривошип	*kreevoship*
gear change	цепная передача	*tsipnahya pirreedarcha*
wire	проволочка	*prorvulluchka*
dynamo	динамо	*deenahma*
frame	рама	*rarma*
dress guard	сетка	*syetka*
chain	цепь	*tsep*
chain guard	кожух	*kuzhookh*
chain lock	велосипедный замок	*vilosipyedny zummork*
milometer	дистанционный спидометр	*distuntsiorny speedormetr*
child's seat	детское седло	*dyetskoyeh sidlor*
headlamp	передний фонарь	*piryaydnee funnar*
bulb	лампочка	*larmpuchka*
pedal	педаль	*pidarl*
pump	насос	*nussorss*
reflector	рефлектор	*riflyektur*

break pad	тормозная колодка	*turmuznahya kullortka*
brake cable	тормозной трос	*turmuznoy trorss*
ring lock	кольцевой замок	*kultsivoy zummork*
carrier straps	резинки	*rizeenki*
tachometer	спидометр	*speedormetr*
spoke	спица	*speetsa*
mudguard	крыло	*krylor*
handlebar	руль	*rool*
chain wheel	зубчатое колесо	*zoopchartoye kullissor*
toe clip	опора для пальцев ног	*uppora dlya parltsiv nork*
crank axle	педальная ось	*pidarlnaya orss*
drum brake	барабанный тормоз	*burrubbarny tormuss*
rim	обод колеса	*orbut kullissar*
valve	вентиль	*vyentil*
valve tube	вентильный шланг	*vyentilny shlank*
gear cable	передаточный трос	*pirreedartuchny trorss*
fork	вилка переднего колеса	*veelka piryaydnyiva kullissar*
front wheel	переднее колесо	*piryaydnyeyeh kullissor*
seat	седло	*idlor*

5.10 Hitchhiking

● **Hitchhiking** as such should be avoided at all costs and outside the main cities it is in principle not permitted. In major cities use officially marked taxis and do not share them with strangers. short-distance lifts may be possible in the provinces, but often the drivers regard their cars as unofficial taxis and expect payment, in which case agree the price in advance.

Where are you heading? _	**Куда вы едете?**
	*Koodar vy **yay**dyetyeh?*
Can I come along? _____	**Вы меня не подвезёте?**
	*Vy min**ya** nyeh puddviz**yo**tyeh?*
I'm trying to get to... _____	**Мне нужно в...**
	*Mnyeh no**o**zhna v...*
How much will you _____ charge (about)?	**Сколько стоит (приблизительно)?**
	*Sk**or**lka st**or**-eet (preebleez**ee**tyilna)?*
Could you drop me off...?	**Вы можете меня высадить в...?**
	*Vy m**or**zhityeh min**ya** vysuddeet v...?*
– here? _____	**Вы можете меня высадить здесь?**
	*Vy m**or**zhityeh min**ya** vysuddeet zdyess?*
– in the centre _____	**Вы можете меня высадить в центре?**
	*Vy m**or**zhityeh min**ya** vysuddeet v ts**ent**ryeh?*
Could you stop _____ here please?	**Остановитесь здесь, пожалуйста**
	*Ustunnuv**ee**tyes zdyess, puzh**ar**looysta*
I'd like to get out here ___	**Я хочу здесь выйти**
	*Ya khuch**oo** zdyess v**y**ti*
Thanks for the lift _____	**Спасибо, что подвезли**
	*Spass**ee**bo, shtor puddvizl**ee***

6.1 In general 82

6.2 Questions to passengers 84

6.3 Tickets 86

6.4 Information 88

6.5 Aeroplanes 90

6.6 Taxis 91

6.1 In general

● **Most tourists** go to Russia with an organised party. People who wish to depart from their programme to make, for example, a journey by train, aeroplane or boat, should consult their tour organisers. Payment for longer journeys will probably be in a foreign currency. It is not known whether aircraft maintenance procedures for domestic flights are always properly observed.

Announcements

Поезд на...,время отправления ...,задерживается на...минут...	The train to...at...has been delayed by...minutes
На путь...прибывает поезд на.../из...	The train now arriving at platform...is the train to .../from...
На пути...продолжается посадка на поезд на...	The train to...is still waiting at platform...
Поезд на...отбывает сегодня с...пути	The train to...will leave from platform...
Мы приближаемся к станции...	We're now approaching...

Where does this train ____ go to?	**Куда идёт этот поезд?**
	Koodar eedyot etut por-yest?
Does this boat go to...? ___	**Этот теплоход идёт в...?**
	Etut tyiplukhort eedyot v...?
Can I take this bus to...? _	**Могу я на этом автобусе доехать до...?**
	Muggoo ya na etum aftorboosye du-yekhat doh...?
Does this train stop at...?	**Этот поезд останавливается в...?**
	Etut por-yest ustunarvleevahyetsa v...?
Is this seat taken/free/ ____ reserved?	**Это место занято/свободно/заказано?**
	Eta myesta zarnyutta/svubbordna/ zukkarzunna?
I've booked... _____	**Я заказывал(а)...**
	Ya zukkarzyval(a)...
Could you tell me _____ where I have to get off for... ?	**Вы не подскажете, где мне выйти для...?**
	Vy nyeh puddskarzhityeh, gdyeh mnyeh vyti dlya...?
Could you let me_____ know when we get to...?	**Вы предупредите меня, когда мы будем у...?**
	Vy pridooprideetyeh minya, kugdah my boodyem oo...?
Could you stop at the ____ next stop, please?	**Остановитесь, пожалуйста, на следующей остановке**
	Ustunnuvveetyes, puzharlooysta, nah slaydooyushchiy ustunnorfkyeh
Where are we now? _____	**Где мы?**
	Gdyeh my?
Do I have to get off here?	**Мне здесь выходить?**
	Mnyeh zdyess vykhuddeet?

6.2 Questions to passengers

Ticket types

Первый класс или второй класс?	First or second class?
В один конец или туда и обратно?	Single or return?
Место для курящих или нет?	Smoking or non-smoking?
У окна или у прохода?	Window or aisle?
Спереди или сзади?	Front or back?
Сидячее или спальное место?	Seat or couchette?
Наверху, посередине или внизу?	Top, middle or bottom?
Туристский класс или бизнес-класс?	Tourist class or business class?
Каюта или сидячее место?	Cabin or seat?
Одноместная или двухместная?	Single or double?
Сколько вас?	How many are travelling?

Have we already _____ passed...?	**Мы уже проехали...?** *My oozheh pruyekhali...?*
How long have I been ___ asleep?	**Сколько я проспал (проспала)?** *Skorlka ya prusparl (pruspullah)?*
How long does... _____ stop here?	**Сколько времени...простоит здесь?** *Skorlka vraymini...prustuh-eet zdyess?*
Can I come back on the _ same ticket?	**Можно по этому билету проехать обратно?** *Morzhno po etummoo beelyetoo pruhyekhat ubbrartno?*
Can I change on this ____ ticket?	**Можно сделать пересадку с этим билетом?** *Morzhno zdyelat pireesartkoo seteem beelyetum?*
How long is this ticket ___ valid for?	**Сколько времени действителен этот билет?** *Skorlka vraymini dyaystveetyelyen etut beelyet?*

Destination

Куда вы едете?	Where are you travelling?
Когда вы отъезжаете?	When are you leaving?
Ваш...отправляется в...	Your...leaves at...
Вам нужно сделать пересадку	You have to change trains
Вам нужно выйти в...	You have to get off at...
Вам нужно проехать через...	You have to travel via...
Поездка туда в...	The outward journey is on...
Поездка обратно в...	The return journey is on...
Вы должны быть на борту не позже...	You have to be on board by...

Inside the vehicle

Biletiniz lütfen	Your ticket, please
Yer ayxrdxJxnxzx gösteren belge lütfen	Your reservation, please
Pasaportunuz lütfen	Your passport, please
Yanlx± yere oturmu±sunuz	You're in the wrong seat
Yanlx± ... binmi±siniz	You're on/in the wrong...
Bu yer ayxrtxlmx±txr	This seat is reserved
Bir miktar ek olarak ödemeniz gerekiyor	You'll have to pay a supplement
... ...dakika rötarlx	The...has been delayed by...minutes

6.3 Tickets

Where can I...?	**Где можно...?**
	Gdyeh morzhno...?
– buy a ticket?	**Где можно купить билет?**
	Gdyeh morzhno koopeet beelyet?
– make a reservation?	**Где можно заказать место?**
	Gdyeh morzhno zukkuzzart myesta?
– book a flight?	**Где можно купить билет на самолёт?**
	Gdyeh morzhno koopeet beelyet nah summalyot?
Could I have a...to..., please?	**Можно мне...в...?**
	Morzhna mnyeh...v...?
– a single	**Можно мне билет в один конец в ...?**
	Morzhna mnyeh beelyet v uddeen kunnyets v...?

– a return _____	Можно мне билет туда и обратно?
	Morzhna mnyeh beelyet toodar ee ubbrartno?
first class _____	первый класс
	pyairvy klarss
second class _____	второй класс
	fturroy klarss
tourist class _____	туристский класс
	tooreestski klarss
business class _____	бизнес-класс
	beezniss-klarss
I'd like to book a _____ seat/couchette/cabin	Я хочу заказать сидячее место/спальное место/каюту
	Ya khuchoo zukkuzzart seedyahcheeyeh myesta/sparlnoye myesta/kayootoo
I'd like to book a berth in the sleeping car	Я хочу заказать место в спальном вагоне
	Ya khuchoo zukkuzzart myesta fsparlnum vuggornyeh
top/middle/bottom _____	наверху/посередине/внизу
	nuvvirkhoo/pussireedeenyeh/vneezoo
smoking/no smoking _____	для курящих/некурящих
	dlya kooryahshchikh/nyehkooryahshchikh
by the window _____	у окна
	oo ukknar
single/double _____	одноместный/двухместный
	uddnamyestny/dvookhmyestny
at the front/back _____	спереди/сзади
	spayridee/s-zardi
There are...of us _____	Нас...человек
	Narss...chilovyek
a car _____	машина
	mushina
a caravan _____	автоприцеп/караван/фургон
	afftapreetsep/kurruvvarn/foorgorn
...bicycles _____	...велосипедов
	...vilussipyeduff

Do you also have...?_____	**У вас есть также...?**
	Oo vuss yest tarkzheh...?
– season tickets? _____	**У вас есть также билет для**
	многократного использования?
	Oo vuss yest tarkzheh beelyet dlya
	mnorgakrartnuvva eesporlzuvvarniya?
– weekly tickets?_____	**У вас есть также абонемент на неделю?**
	Oo vuss yest tarkzheh abunnimyent nah
	nidyaylyu?
– monthly tickets?_____	**У вас есть также абонемент на месяц?**
	Oo vuss yest tarkzheh abunnimyent nah
	myaysyets?

6.4 Information

Where's...? _____	**Где...?**
	Gdyeh...?
Where's the information__ desk?	**Где информационная служба?**
	Gdyeh eenformatseeornaya sloozhba?
Where's the indicator _____ board?	**Где табло прибытия/отправления?**
	Gdyeh tubblor preebyteeya/uttpruvvl
	yayniya?
Where's the...desk? _____	**Где стол...?**
	Gdyeh storl...?
Do you have a city map__ with the bus/the underground routes on it?	**У вас есть план города с указанием**
	автобусов/метро?
	Oo vuss yest plarn gorudda sookuzarniyem
	aftorboossoff/mitror?
Do you have a _____ timetable?	**У вас есть расписание?**
	Oo vuss yest russpeesarneeya?
I'd like to confirm/_____ cancel/change my booking for/trip to...	**Я хочу подтвердить/аннулировать/**
	переменить заказ билета в...
	Ya khuchoo puddtveerdeet/anooleeruvat/
	peerimineet zukkarss beelyeta v...

Will I get my money _____ back?	**Я могу получить деньги обратно?**
	Ya muggoo pulloocheet dyengi ubbrartna?
I want to go to... _____ How do I get there? (What's the quickest way there?)	**Мне нужно в...как мне (быстрее) туда доехать?**
	Mnyeh noozhna v...Kukk mnyeh (bystrayeh) toodar duh-yekhat?
How much is a _____ single/return to...?	**Сколько стоит билет в один конец в...?/ Сколько стоит билет туда и обратно в...?**
	Skorlka stor-eet beelyet vuddeen kunnyets v...?/Skorlka stor-eet beelyet toodar ee ubbrartna v...?
Do I have to pay a _____ supplement?	**Мне нужно доплатить?**
	Mnyeh noozhnah dupplutteet?
Can I interrupt my _____ journey with this ticket?	**Могу я прервать путешествие с этим билетом?**
	Muggoo ya prairvat pootyeshestviya setim beelyetum?
How much luggage _____ am I allowed?	**Сколько можно взять багажа с собой?**
	Skorlka morzhna vzyart buggazhar s-subboy?
Does this...travel direct? _	**Идёт...прямо туда?**
	Eedyot...pryarma toodar?
Do I have to change? _____ Where?	**Мне нужно пересаживаться? Где?**
	Mnyeh noozhna pireesarzhivartsa? Gdyeh?
Will there be any _____ stopovers?	**Самолёт делает промежуточные посадки?**
	Summullyot dyelayet prummizhootuchny-yeh pusatki?
Does the boat call in at _ any ports on the way?	**Пароход заходит по дороге в гавани?**
	Purrukhort zukhordit puh durrorgye v garvani?
Does the train/ _____ bus stop at...?	**Поезд/автобус останавливается в...?**
	Por-yist/aftorbus ustunarvlivahyetsya v...?
Where should I get off? _	**Где мне выходить?**
	Gdyeh mnyeh vykhuddeet?

Is there a connection ____ to...?	**Существует связь в...?** *Sooshchistvooyet svyaz v...?*
How long do I have to ____ wait?	**Сколько мне ждать?** *Skorlka mnyeh zhdart?*
When does...leave? ____	**Когда отходит...?** *Kugdar utkhordit...?*
What time does the ____ first/next/last...leave?	**Во сколько идёт первый/следующий/последний...?** *Va skorlka eedyot pyairvy/ slyaydooyushchi/pusslyaydni...?*
How long does...take? ____	**Сколько времени находится...в пути?** *Skorlka vraymini nukhorditsa...fpootee?*
What time does...arrive __ in...?	**Во сколько приходит...в...?** *Va skorlka preekhordit...v...?*
Where does the...to... ____ leave from?	**Откуда отходит...в...?** *Utkoodah uttkhordit...v...?*
Is this...to...? ____	**Этот...идёт в...?** *Etut...eedyot v...?*

6.5 Aeroplanes

● **At arrival at a Russian airport** (аэропорт), you will find the following signs:

прилёт arrivals **отлёт/вылет** departures	**внутренние полёты** domestic flights	**международный** international

6.6 Taxis

свободно for hire	занято booked	стоянка такси taxi rank

Taxi! _____	**такси!** *Tuksee!*
Could you get me a taxi, _ please?	**Вы можете заказать для меня такси?** *Vy morzhitye zukkuzzart dlya minya tuksee?*
Where can I find a taxi ___ around here?	**Где здесь можно поймать такси?** *Gdyeh zdyess morzhna puymart tuksee?*
Could you take me to..., _ please?	**Отвезите меня, пожалуйста, в...** *Utvizeetye minya, puzharlooysta, v...*
– this address _____	**Отвезите меня, пожалуйста, по этому адресу** *Utvizeetye minya, puzharlooysta, po etummoo ardrissoo*
– the...hotel _____	**Отвезите меня, пожалуйста, в гостиницу** *Utvizeetye minya, puzharlooysta, v gusteenitsoo*
– the town/city centre ___	**Отвезите меня, пожалуйста, в центр** *Utvizeetye minya, puzharlooysta, v tsentr*
– the station _____	**Отвезите меня, пожалуйста, на вокзал** *Utvizeetye minya, puzharlooysta, nah vukkzarl*
– the airport _____	**Отвезите меня, пожалуйста, в аэропорт** *Utvizeetye minya, puzharlooysta, vairoport*
How much is the_____ trip to...?	**Сколько стоит поездка в...?** *Skorlka stor-eet pu-yestka v...?*
How far is it to...? _____	**Как далеко до...?** *Kukk dullikor doh...?*
Could you turn on the ___ meter, please?	**Включите, пожалуйста, счётчик** *Fklyoocheetye, puzharlooysta, shchotchik*

I'm in a hurry _____	Я тороплюсь
	Ya turruplyoos
Could you speed up/ _____ slow down a little?	Вы можете ехать побыстрее/помедленнее?
	Vy morzhitye yekhat pubystray-yeh/pomaydlinyayeh?
Could you take a_____ different route?	Вы можете поехать по другой дороге?
	Vy morzhitye puh-yekhat po droogoy durrorgye?
I'd like to get out here,___ please	Высадите меня здесь
	Vysadeetyeh minya zdyess
You have to go straight __ on here	Вам нужно здесь ехать прямо
	Varm noozhna zdyess yekhat pryarma
You have to turn left_____ here	Вам нужно здесь повернуть налево
	Varm noozhna zdyess puvirnoot nullyeva
You have to turn right____ here	Вам нужно здесь повернуть направо
	Varm noozhna zdyess puvirnoot nuprarva
This is it _____	Это здесь
	Eto zdyess
Could you wait a minute _ for me, please?	Вы можете меня минутку подождать?
	Vy morzhitye minya minootkoo pudduzhdart?

7.1 General 94

7.2 Camping 95

Camping equipment 98

7.3 Hotel/B&B/apartment/holiday house 100

7.4 Complaints 102

7.5 Departure 104

7.1 General

● **Going to Russia** on the off-chance and booking hotels when there is still difficult. Most people go as members of a party or as individuals on business and all visa and accommodation arrangements in hotels or campsites are made in advance from Britain.

My name's...I've made ___ a reservation over the phone/by mail	**Моя фамилия...я заказывал(а) место (по телефону/письменно)**
	Muyah fameeliya...ya zukkarzyval(a) myesta (po tyelifornoo/peesminna)
How much is it per ___ night/week/ month?	**Сколько стоит в день/неделю/месяц?**
	Skorlka stor-eet vdyen/nidyaylyu/myaysits?
We'll be staying at ___ least...nights/weeks.	**Мы пробудем по крайней мере...дней/недель**
	My prubboodyem po krigh-nyay myairyeh...dnyay/nidyayl
We don't know yet ___	**Мы ещё точно не знаем**
	My yishchor torchna nyeh znah-yem
Do you allow pets ___ (cats/dogs)?	**Вы допускаете домашних животных (собак/кошек)?**
	Vy duppooskah-yetyeh dummarshnikh zhivortnykh (subbark/korshik)?

Сколько вы пробудете?	How long will you be staying?
Заполните этот бланк, пожалуйста	Fill in this form, please
Ваш паспорт, пожалуйста	Could I see your passport?
Вам нужно заплатить залог	I'll need a deposit
Вам нужно заплатить вперёд	You'll have to pay in advance

What time does the _____ gate/door open/close?	Во сколько вы открываете/закрываете ворота/дверь?
	Vo skorlka vy utkryvahyetyeh/ zukryvahyetye vurrorta/dvyair?
Could you get me _____ a taxi, please?	Закажите для меня, пожалуйста, такси
	Zukkuzheetyeh dlya minya, puzharlooysta, tuksee
Is there any mail _____ for me?	Есть почта для меня?
	Yest porchta dlya minya?

7.2 Camping

Where's the manager? ___	Где заведующий?
	Gdyeh zuvvyaydooyushchi?
Are we allowed to _____ camp here?	Мы можем здесь поставить палатку?
	My morzhim zdyess pustarveet pullartkoo?
There are...of us and ____ ...tents	Нас...человек и...палаток
	Narss...chillovyek ee...pullartuk
Can we pick our _____ own site?	Мы можем сами выбрать место?
	My morzhim sarmi vybrat myesta?

Вы можете сами выбрать место	You can pick your own site
Вам укажут место	You'll be allocated a site
Вот номер вашего места	This is your site number
Наклейте это на вашу машину, пожалуйста	Stick this on your car, please
Не потеряйте эту карточку, пожалуйста	Please don't lose this card

Do you have a quiet _____ spot for us?

У вас есть тихое местечко для нас?

*Oo vuss **yest** teekhoyeh mistyechka dlya narss?*

Do you have any other ____ sites available?

У вас нет другого свободного места?

*Oo vuss **nyet** droogorva svubbordnuvva myesta?*

It's too windy/sunny/ _____ shady here

Здесь слишком сильный ветер/Здесь слишком солнечно/Здесь слишком много тени

Zdyess sleeshkum seelny vyaytyer/Zdyess sleeshkum sorlnichna/Zdyess sleeshkum mnorga tyayni

It's too noisy here _____

Здесь слишком шумно

Zdyess sleeshkum shoomna

The ground's too _____ hard/uneven

Земля слишком твёрдая/неровная

Zimlyah sleeshkum tvyordaya/nirorvnaya

Do you have a level _____ spot for the camper/caravan/tents?

У вас есть горизонтальное место для кемпера/каравана/ складного каравана?

*Oo vuss **yest** gurreezuntarlnoye myesta dlya kyempera/kurruvarna/ skludnorva kurruvarna?*

Could we have adjoining _ pitches?

Мы можем стоять рядом?

My morzhim stuyart ryardum?

Can we park the car_____ next to the tent?

Можно поставить машину около палатки?

Morzhna pustarvit mashinoo orkulla pullartki?

How much is it per _____ person/tent/caravan/car?

Сколько стоит на человека/палатку/караван/машину?

Skorlka stor-it nah chillovyeka/ pullartkoo/kurruvvarn/mushinoo?

Do you have any _____ bungalows for hire?

Вы сдаёте домики?

Vy zdayotyeh dormeeki?

Are there any...? _____

Есть ли...?

Yest-lee...?

– hot showers? _____	**Есть ли душ с горячей водой?** *Yest-lee doosh zgurryahchi vuddoy?*
– washing machines?____	**Есть ли стиральные машины?** *Yest-lee steerarlny-yeh mashiny?*
Is there a...on the site? __	**Есть на территории...?** *Yest nah territorii...?*
Is there a children's_____ play area on the site?	**Есть на территории детская площадка?** *Yest nah territorii dyetskaya plushchartka?*
Are there covered _____ cooking facilities on the site?	**Есть на территории крытое место для** **приготовления пищи?** *Yest nah territorii krytoyeh myesta dlya* *preeguttuvlyayniya peeshchi?*
Can I rent a safe here? __	**Можно здесь снять сейф?** *Morzhna zdyess snyart syayf?*
Are we allowed to _____ barbecue here?	**Здесь можно разжечь барбекю?** *Zdyess morzhna ruz-zhaych barbikyoo?*
Are there any power _____ points?	**Здесь есть электрические розетки?** *Zdyess yest eliktreechiskeeyeh ruzzetki?*
Is there drinking water? __	**Здесь есть питьевая вода?** *Zdyess yest peetyevahya vuddar?*
When's the rubbish_____ collected?	**Когда собирают мусор?** *Kugdah subbeerahyut moossur?*
Do you sell gas bottles __ (butane gas/propane gas)?	**Вы продаёте баллоны с газом** **(бутан/пропан)?** *Vy prudda-yotyeh bullorny zgarzum* *(bootarn/prupparn)?*
Do you have a _____ single/double room available?	**У вас есть одноместный/двухместный** **номер?** *Oo vuss yest odnomyestny/dvookhmyestny* *normer?*

Camping equipment

luggage space	место для багажа	*myesta dlya bugguzhar*
can opener	открывалка	*utkryvarlka*
butane gas	баллон с бутаном	*ballorn zbootarnum*
pannier	велосипедная сумка	*vilossipyednaya soomka*
gas cooker	газовая плитка	*garzuvvaya pleetka*
groundsheet	дно палатки	*dnor pullartki*
mallet	молоток	*mulluttork*
hammock	гамак	*gamark*
jerry can	канистра	*kaneestra*
campfire	костёр	*kustyor*
folding chair	складной стул	*skludnoy stool*
insulated picnic box	сумка-холодильник	*soomka-khulludeelnik*
ice pack	охлаждающий элемент	*okhluzhdahyushchi ellimyent*
compass	компас	*kormpus*
wick	фитиль	*feeteel*
corkscrew	штопор	*shtorpor*
airbed	надувной матрац	*nudoovnoy mutrats*
airbed plug	затычка от надувного матраца	*zuttychka ut nudoovnorva mutratsa*
pump	воздушный насос	*vuzdooshny nussorss*
awning	навес	*nuvyess*
karimat	коврик	*korvreek*
pan	кастрюля	*kustryoolya*
pan handle	ручка кастрюли	*roochka kustryooli*
primus stove	примус	*preemoos*
zip	молния	*morlniya*
backpack	рюкзак	*ryookzark*
guy rope	тяговый канат	*tyarguvvy kunnart*
sleeping bag	спальный мешок	*sparlny mishork*

storm lantern	фонарь "молния"	funnar "morlniya"
camp bed	раскладушка	russkluddooshka
table	стол	storl
tent	палатка	pullartka
tent peg	колышек	korlyshek
tent pole	палка	parlka
vacuum flask	термос	tairmus
water bottle	фляжка	flyashka
clothes peg	прищепка	preeshchepka
clothes line	бельевая верёвка	bilyevahya viryofka
windbreak	ветровой щит	vitruvvoy shcheet
torch	карманный фонарь	kurrmarny funnar
pocket knife	складной нож	skludnoy norzh

7.3 Hotel/B&B/apartment/holiday house

Туалет и душ на том же этаже/ в вашем номере	You can find the toilet and shower on the same floor/en suite
Сюда, пожалуйста	This way, please
Ваша комната на...этаже, номер...	Your room is on the...floor, number...

Do you have a _____ single/double room available?	**У вас есть одноместный/двухместный номер?** *Oo vuss yest odnom**yes**tny/dvookhm**yes**tny n**o**rmer?*
per person/per room _____	**с человека/за номер** *schilluvv**ye**ka/zah n**o**rmer*
Does that include _____ breakfast/lunch/dinner?	**Это включая завтрак/обед/ ужин?** *Eto fklyuch**a**hya z**a**rftruk/**u**bb**yet**/**oo**zhin?*
Could we have two_____ adjoining rooms?	**Мы можем снять два номера рядом?** *My m**o**rzhim snyart dvah n**o**rmera ry**ar**dum?*
with/without _____ toilet/bath/shower	**с туалетом/ванной/душем; без туалета/ванны/душа** *s tooull**yet**um/v**a**rnoy/d**oo**shem; byes tooull**ye**ta/v**a**rny/d**oo**sha*
(not) facing the street _____	**(не) выходящий на улицу** *(nyeh) vykhud**ya**shchi nah **oo**litsu*
with/without a view_____ of the sea	**с видом на море/без вида на море** *sv**ee**dum nah m**o**ryeh/byez v**ee**da nah m**o**ryeh*
Is there...in the hotel?_____	**Есть в гостинице...?** *Yest vgust**ee**nitseh...?*
Is there a lift in the _____ hotel?	**Есть в гостинице лифт?** *Yest vgust**ee**nitseh leeft?*

Could I see the room? ___	**Можно посмотреть номер?**
	Morzhna pusmutrayt normer?
I'll take this room_____	**Я сниму этот номер**
	Ya sneemoo etut normer
We don't like this one____	**Этот номер нам не нравится**
	Etut normer nahm nyeh nrarvitsa
Do you have a larger/____ less expensive room?	**У вас есть номер побольше?/У вас есть номер подешевле?**
	Oo vuss yest normer pubborlsheh?/Oo vuss yest normer puddishevlyeh?
Could you put in a cot? __	**Вы можете поставить детсткую кроватку?**
	Vy morzhityeh pustarvit dyetskooyu kruvartkoo?
What time's breakfast? __	**Во сколько завтрак?**
	Vuh skorlko zarftruk?
Where's the dining _____ room?	**Где столовая?**
	Gdyeh stullorvaya?
Can I have breakfast ____ in my room?	**Вы можете принести завтрак в номер?**
	Vy morzhityeh preenistee zarftruk vnormer?
Where's the emergency __ exit/fire escape?	**Где запасной выход/пожарная лестница?**
	Gdyeh zuppusnoy vykhud/puzharnaya lyesnitsa?
Where can I park my ____ car (safely)?	**Где можно надёжно поставить машину?**
	Gdyeh morzhna nudyozhna pustarveet mushinoo?
The key to room..., _____ please	**Ключ от номера..., пожалуйста**
	Klyooch ut normera..., puzharlooysta
Could you put this in ____ the safe, please?	**Можно положить это в сейф?**
	Morzhna pulluzheet eto fsayf?
Could you wake me _____ at...tomorrow?	**Разбудите меня завтра в...часов, пожалуйста**
	Razboodeetyeh minya zarftra v...chussorf, puzharlooysta

Could you find a _____ babysitter for me?	Вы можете найти мне няню для ребёнка?
	Vy morzhitye nigh-tee mnyeh nyarnyu dlya ribyonka?
Could I have an extra____ blanket?	У вас есть ещё одеяло?
	Oo vuss yest yishchor uddiyahla?
What days do the _____ cleaners come in?	По каким дням производится уборка?
	Po kukkeem dnyam pruh-eezvorditsa ooborka?
When are the sheets/____ towels/tea towels changed?	Когда меняют постельное бельё/полотенца/кухонные полотенца?
	Kugdar minyahyut pustyelnoye bilyor/pullutyentsa/kookhunny-yeh pullutyentsa?

7.4 Complaints

We can't sleep for_____ the noise	Мы не можем спать из-за шума
	My nyeh morzhim spart eez-zah shooma
Could you turn the _____ radio down, please?	Нельзя ли сделать радио потише?
	Nilzyar lee zdyelat rahdio putteesheh?
We're out of toilet paper _	Кончилась туалетная бумага
	Korncheelas tooullyetnaya boomarga
There aren't any.../there's not enough...	Нет/недостаточно...
	Nyet/nidustartuchna...
The bed linen's dirty_____	Постельное бельё грязное
	Pustyelnoye bilyor gryahznoyeh
The room hasn't been ___ cleaned.	Комната не убрана
	Kormnutta nyeh oobrunna
The kitchen is not clean__	Кухня не убрана
	Kookhnya nyeh oobrunna
The kitchen utensils are__ dirty	Кухонные принадлежности грязные
	Kookhunny-yeh preenudlyezhnusti gryahzny-yeh

The heater's not _____ working	**Отопление не работает**
	Uttuplayniyeh nyeh rubbortayet
There's no (hot) _____ water/electricity	**Нет (горячей) воды/электричества**
	Nyet (gurryahchi) vuddy/eliktreechistva
...is broken _____	**...сломан(а)**
	...slorman(a)
Could you have that _____ seen to?	**Вы можете это починить?**
	Vy morzhitye eto puchineet?
Could I have another _____ room/site?	**Можно другой номер?/Можно другое место для палатки?**
	Morzhna droogoy normer? Morzhna droogoryeh myesta dlya pullartki?
The bed creaks terribly __	**Кровать ужасно скрипит**
	Kruvvart oozharsna skripeet
The bed sags_____	**Кровать очень прогибается**
	Kruvvart orchin pruggibahyetsa
There are insects/ _____ bedbugs in our room	**Нас одолевают насекомые/клопы**
	Nahs uddullivahyut nussikormy-yeh/kluppy
This place is full_____ of mosquitos	**Здесь полно комаров**
	Zdyess pulnor kummaroff
– cockroaches _____	**Здесь полно тараканов**
	Zdyess pulnor turrukkarnuff

7.5 Departure

See also 8.2 Settling the bill

I'm leaving tomorrow.____ Could I settle my bill, please?	Я уезжаю завтра. Рассчитайте меня, пожалуйста *Ya ooyiz-zhahyoo zarftra. Rus-schitigh-tyeh minya, puzharlooysta*
What time should we ____ vacate?	Во сколько мы должны покинуть...? *Va skorlka my dulzhny pukkeenoot...?*
Could I have my deposit/ passport back, please?	Можно получить залог/паспорт обратно? *Morzhna pulloocheet zullork/parsspurt ubbrartna?*
We're in a terrible hurry ___	Мы очень торопимся *My orchin turrorpimsya*
Could you forward _____ my mail to this address?	Вы можете пересылать мою почту по этому адресу? *Vy morzhityeh peerisylart muyoo porchtoo po etummoo ardrisoo?*
Could we leave our_____ luggage here until we leave?	Можно оставить чемоданы здесь до нашего отъезда? *Morzhna ustarveet chimuddarny zdyess duh narshivo utyezda?*
Thanks for your _____ hospitality	Спасибо за гостеприимство *Spasseebo zah gustipree-eemstva*

8 Money matters

8.1 Banks 106

8.2 Settling the bill 107

● **It is not permitted** to take roubles into or out of Russia. Tourists should take mint-condition foreign currency notes or travellers cheques. Some bank cards can be used at cash machines and in shops in major cities. Cheques are not usually accepted. *Bureaux de change* can be found in hotels, airports, banks and other places. When you change money you must present your passport and declaration form.

8.1 Banks

Распишитесь здесь	Sign here, please
Заполните это	Fill this out, please
Покажите, пожалуйста, паспорт	Could I see your passport, please?
Покажите, пожалуйста удостоверение личности	Could I see some identification, please?

Where can I find a_____ bank/an exchange office around here?	**Где здесь поблизости банк/обмен валюты?**
	Gdyeh zdyess publeezusti barnk/ubmyen vullyooty?
Where can I cash this_____ traveller's cheque/giro cheque?	**Где можно поменять этот чек?**
	Gdyeh morzhna pumminyart etut chek?
Can I cash this...here? ___	**Можно здесь поменять...?**
	Morzhna zdyess pumminyart...?
Can I withdraw money ___ on my credit card here?	**Можно получить деньги по кредитной карточке?**
	Morzhna pulloocheet dyengee po kredeetnoy kartuchkeh?
What's the minimum/ ___ maximum amount?	**Каков минимум/максимум?**
	Kukkorff meeneemum/markseemum?

Can I take out less than that?	**Можно получить меньше?**
	Morzhna pulloocheet myensheh?
I've had some money transferred here. Has it arrived yet?	**Мне перевели деньги по телеграфу. Они уже пришли?**
	Mnyeh pirrivillee dyengi po tyelligrarfoo. Unnee oozheh preeshlee?
These are the details of my bank in the UK	**Вот данные моего банка в Великобритании/Англии**
	Vot darny-yeh muyivvor barnka v Villeekobritarnii/Arnglii
I'd like to change some money	**Я хочу поменять деньги**
	Ya khuchoo pumminyat dyengi
– pounds into...	**Английские фунты на...**
	Ungleeskiyeh foonty nah...
– dollars into...	**Американские доллары на...**
	Ummerikarnskiyeh dorlary nah...
What's the exchange rate?	**Какой валютный курс?**
	Kukkoy vullyootny koorss?
Could you give me some small change with it?	**Вы можете дать мне часть мелочью?**
	Vy morzhityeh dart mnyeh charst myeluchyu?
This is not right	**Это неправильно**
	Eto niprarvilna

8.2 Settling the bill

Could you put it on my bill?	**Запишите на мой счёт, пожалуйста**
	Zuppisheetyeh nah moy schot, puzharlooysta
Does this amount include service?	**Это включая обслуживание?**
	Eto fklyoochahya ubsloozhivarniyeh?
Can I pay by...?	**Можно заплатить ...?**
	Morzhna zupplutteet ...?
Can I pay by credit card?	**Можно заплатить кредитной карточкой?**
	Morzhna zupplutteet kredeetnoy kartuchkoy?

Can I pay by traveller's __ cheque?	**Можно заплатить дорожным чеком?** *Morzhna zupplutteet durrorzhnym chekum?*
Can I pay with foreign ___ currency?	**Можно заплатить иностранной валютой?** *Morzhna zupplutteet eenustrarnoy valyootoy?*
You've given me too_____ much/you haven't given me enough change	**Вы мне дали слишком много/мало сдачи** *Vy mnyeh darli sleeshkum mnorga/marla zdarchi*
Could you check this ____ again, please?	**Пересчитайте это, пожалуйста** *Pirrischitigh-tyeh eto, puzharlooysta*
Could I have a receipt,___ please?	**Дайте мне, пожалуйста, квитанцию/чек** *Digh-tyeh mnyeh, puzharlooysta, kveetarntsiyoo/chek*
I don't have enough _____ money on me	**У меня с собой недостаточно денег** *Oo minya s-subboy nidustartuchno dyaynik*
We don't accept credit___ cards/traveller's cheques/foreign currency	**Мы не принимаем кредитные карточки/дорожные чеки/ иностранную валюту** *My nyeh prineemahyem kredeetny-yeh kartuchki/durrorzhny-yeh cheki/eenustrarnooyu valyootoo*
This is for you _____	**Пожалуйста, это вам** *Puzharlooysta, eto varm*
Keep the change_____	**Оставьте сдачу себе** *Ustarvtye zdarchoo sibyeh*

9

Post and telephone

9.1 Post 110

9.2 Telephone 112

9.1 Post

● **Post offices** can also arrange telephone calls and faxes (they have special branches for international calls). Giro cheques are not accepted for payment. Large hotels have agencies that sell stamps, wrap and despatch parcels, and also send faxes. Letterboxes in the street are blue.

посылки parcels	**марки** stamps	**телеграммы** telegrams
почтовые переводы money order		

Where's...? _____	**Где...?** *Gdyeh?*
Where's the post office? _	**Где здесь поблизости почта?** *Gdyeh zdyess publeezusti porchta?*
Where's the main post office?	**Где главный почтамт?** *Gdyeh glarvny puchtarmt?*
Where's the postbox? ____	**Где здесь поблизости почтовый ящик?** *Gdyeh zdyess publeezusti puchtorvy yarshchik?*
Which counter should I go to...?	**В каком окне можно...?** *Fkukkorm uknyeh morzhna...?*
– to change money_____	**В каком окне можно поменять деньги?** *Fkukkorm uknyeh morzhna pumminyaht dyengi?*
– for a Telegraph Money Order?	**В каком окне можно переслать деньги по телеграфу?** *Fkukkorm uknyeh morzhna pireeslart dyengi po tyeligrarfoo?*
Poste restante _____	**До востребования** *Doh vustraybuvvarniya*

Is there any mail for me? My name's...	**Есть почта для меня? Моя фамилия...** *Yest porchta dlya minya? Mu-ya fameeliya...*

Stamps

What's the postage for a...to...?	**Какие марки нужны для...в...?** *Kukkee-yeh marki noozhny dlya...v...?*
Are there enough stamps on it?	**Достаточно марок?** *Dustartuchno marukk?*
I'd like... ...rouble stamps	**...марок ценой...,пожалуйста** *...marukk tsinoy..., puzharlooysta*
I'd like to send this...	**Я хочу отправить это...** *Ya khuchoo utprarvit eto...*
– express	**Я хочу отправить это экспрессом** *Ya khuchoo utprarvit eto ekspryessum*
– by air mail	**Я хочу отправить это авиапочтой** *Ya khuchoo utprarvit eto arviaporchtoy*
– by registered mail	**Я хочу отправить это заказным** *Ya khuchoo utprarvit eto zukkuznym*

Telegram / fax

I'd like to send a telegram to...	**Я хочу отправить телеграмму в...** *Ya khuchoo utprarvit tyeligrarmoo v...*
How much is that per word?	**Сколько стоит одно слово?** *Skorlka stor-eet udnor slorva?*
This is the text I want to send	**Вот текст телеграммы** *Vort tyekst tyeligrarmy*
Shall I fill out the form myself?	**Давайте я заполню бланк сам(а)** *Duvvigh-tyeh ya zupporlnyu blarnk sarm (summar)*
Can I photocopy here?	**Могу я здесь сделать фотокопию?** *Muggoo ya zdyess zdyelat futtakorpiyu?*
Can I send a fax here?	**Могу я здесь отослать факс?** *Muggoo ya zdyess uttuslart farks?*
How much is it per page?	**Сколько стоит за страницу?** *Skorlka stor-eet za strunneetsoo?*

9.2 Telephone

See also 1.8 Telephone alphabet

● **Telephone kiosks** on the street (автоматы, *ufftummarty*) work with tokens (жетоны, *zhetony*) which can be bought at post offices and elsewhere. Trunk calls and international calls can be made direct from private phones and such calls can also be booked in hotels and special branches of post offices.

Is there a phone box _____ around here?	**Здесь есть поблизости телефон-автомат?**
	*Zdyezz **yest** publeezusti tyeliforn-ufftamart?*
Could I use your _____ phone, please?	**Можно воспользоваться вашим телефоном?**
	Morzhna vusporlzuvvartsa varshim tyelifornum?
Do you have a _____ (city/region)...phone directory?	**У вас есть телефонный справочник города .../района...?**
	*Oo vuss **yest** tyeliforny sprarvuchnik gorudda.../right-orna...?*
Where can I get a _____ phone card?	**Дайте мне, пожалуйста,...**
	Digh-tyeh mnyeh, purzharlooysta,...
Could you give me...? ___ the number for international directory enquiries	**Дайте мне, пожалуйста, номер информации для заграницы**
	Digh-tyeh mnyeh, purzharlooysta, normer eenfarmartsii dlya zuggrunneetsy
– the number of room... __	**Дайте мне, пожалуйста, номер комнаты...**
	Digh-tyeh mnyeh, purzharlooysta, normer kormnutty...
– the code _____	**Дайте мне, пожалуйста, код...**
	Digh-tyeh mnyeh, purzharlooysta, kort...
– the number of... _____	**Дайте мне, пожалуйста, номер...**
	Digh-tyeh mnyeh, purzharlooysta, normer...

Could you check if this ___ number's correct?	**Проверьте, пожалуйста, правильность этого номера**
	Pruvvyairtyeh, puzharlooysta, prarvilnust etuvva normera
Do I have to go through___ the switchboard?	**Нужно заказывать через телефонистку?**
	Noozhna zukkarzyvat chayruss tyelifoneestkoo?
Do I have to dial '0' first?	**Нужно ли набрать сначала ноль?**
	Noozhna lee nubbrart snucharla norl?
Do I have to book _____ my calls?	**Нужно ли заказывать разговор?**
	Noozhna lee zukkarzyvart ruzzguvvor?
Could you dial this _____ number for me, please?	**Наберите мне, пожалуйста, этот номер**
	Nabirreetyeh mnyeh, puzharlooysta, etut normer
Could you put me _____ through to.../extension..., please?	**Свяжите меня, пожалуйста, с.../номером...**
	Svyazheetye minya, puzharlooysta, s.../normerum
What's the charge per ___ minute?	**Сколько стоит в минуту?**
	Skorlka stor-eet vminootoo?
Have there been any ___ calls for me?	**Мне кто-нибудь звонил?**
	Mnyeh ktor-neeboot zvunneel?

The conversation

Hello, this is... _____	**Здравствуйте, с вами говорит...**
	Zdrarstvooytyeh, svarmi guvvureet...
Who is this, please? _____	**С кем я говорю?**
	Skyem ya guvvuryoo?
Is this...? _____	**Я говорю с..?**
	Ya guvvuryoo s...?
I'm sorry, I've dialled _____ the wrong number	**Извините, я ошибся/ошиблась номером**
	Eezvinneetyeh, ya ushipsya/ushiblas normerum
I can't hear you _____	**Я вас не слышу**
	Ya vuss nyeh slyshoo

I'd like to speak to..._____	**Я бы хотел(а) поговорить с...**
	Ya by khuttyel(a) pugguvvureet s...
Is there anybody _____ who speaks English?	**Кто-нибудь говорит по-английски?**
	Ktor-niboot guvvureet po-ungleeski?
Extension..., please _____	**Свяжите меня, пожалуйста, с номером...**
	Svyazheetyeh minya, puzharlooysta, snormerum...
Could you ask him/her____ to call me back?	**Попросите его/её перезвонить мне, пожалуйста**
	Pupprusseetyeh yivor/yeyor pirizvunneet mnyeh, puzharlooysta
My name's..._____ My number's...	**Меня зовут.../Мой номер...**
	Minya zuvvoot.../Moy normer
Could you tell him/her ____ I called?	**Передайте, пожалуйста, что я звонил(а)**
	Piridigh-tye, puzharlooysta, shtor ya zvunneel(a)
I'll call back tomorrow ____	**Я позвоню ему/ей завтра**
	Ya puzvunnyoo yimoo/yay zarftra

Вас к телефону	There's a phone call for you
Наберите сначала ноль	You have to dial '0' first
Секундочку	One moment, please
Ничего не слышно	I can't hear anything
Телефон занят	The line's engaged
Вы подождёте?	Do you want to hold?
Соединяю	Putting you through
Вы ошиблись номером	You've got a wrong number
Его/её в данный момент нет	He's/she's not here right now
Он/она будет на месте...	He'll/she'll be back...
Это автоответчик...	This is the answering machine of...

10 Shopping

10.1 Shopping conversations 116

10.2 Food 119

10.3 Clothing and shoes 120

10.4 Photographs and video 122

10.5 At the hairdresser's 125

● **Opening times:** Food shops and markets are open all week, usually from 8.00 a.m. to 9.00 p.m. Other shops usually shut by 8.00 p.m. and have closing days. Foreign currency is not usually accepted, but special foreign currency shops exist. Many shops still have the Soviet system of paying till chits at different counters.

10.1 Shopping conversations

Where can I get...?	В каком магазине я могу купить...?
	Fkukkorm mugguzeenyeh ya muggoo koopeet...?
When does this shop open?	Когда работает этот магазин?
	Kugdar rubbortayet etut mugguzeen?
Could you tell me where the...department is?	Покажите мне, пожалуйста, где отдел...
	Pukkuzheetyeh mnyeh, puzharlooysta, gdyeh utdyel...
Could you help me, please? I'm looking for...	Вы мне не поможете? я ищу...
	Vy mnyeh nyeh pummorzhityeh? Ya eeshchoo...
Do you sell English/ American newspapers?	Вы продаёте английские/американские газеты?
	Vy pruddayotyeh ungleeskiyeh/ummerikarnskiye guzyayty?

Вас уже обслуживают?	Are you being served?

No, I'd like...	Нет. я бы хотел(а)...
	Nyet. Ya by khuttyel(a)...
I'm just looking, if that's all right	Я просто хочу посмотреть, если можно
	Ya prorsta khuchoo pussmutrayt, yesli morzhna

антикварный магазин antiques	**кожгалантерея** leather goods	**спортивные товары** sports shop
аптека pharmacy	**меха** furs	**сувениры/магазин сувениров** souvenirs/souvenir shop
'Берёзка' 'Beryozka' foreign currency shop	**молоко** milk	**табак/табачный магазин** tobacco/tobacconist
булочная/хлеб bakery	**мясо/мясной магазин** meat/butcher's shop	**универмаг** department store
букинистический магазин second-hand book shop	**обувь/магазин обуви** footwear/shoe shop	**фарфор** china
вино/винный магазин off-licence	**овощи-фрукты** greengrocer	**фототовары** camera shop
гастроном delicatessen	**очки, оптика** opticians	**хозяйственные товары** household goods
грампластинки record shop	**парикмахерская(же нская/мужская)** hairdresser (ladies'/men's)	**цветы/цветочный магазин** flowers/flower shop
дамское бельё lingerie	**парфюмерия** perfumery	**электротовары** electrical appliances
игрушки/магазин игрушек toys/toyshop	**посуда** kitchenware shop	**ювелирные изделия** jewellers
канцтовары stationery	**прачечная** laundry	
книги/книжный магазин books/bookshop	**продукты** grocery store	
комиссионный магазин second-hand goods	**ремонт обуви** shoe repairs	
кондитерская cake shop	**рыба/рыбный магазин** fish/fish shop	
	рынок market	

Извините, у нас этого нет	I'm sorry, we don't have that
Извините, всё распродано	I'm sorry, we're sold out
Извините, это поступит снова...	I'm sorry, that won't be in until...
Заплатите в кассе	You can pay at the cash desk
Мы не принимаем кредитные карточки	We don't accept credit cards
Мы не принимаем дорожные чеки	We don't accept traveller's cheques
Мы не принимаем иностранную валюту	We don't accept foreign currency

Что-нибудь ещё?	Anything else?

Yes, I'd also like... _____	Да, мне нужно ещё...
	Dah, mnyeh noozhna yishchor...
No, thank you. That's all _	Нет, спасибо. Это всё
	Nyet, spasseeba. Eto fsyo
Could you show me...? __	Покажите, пожалуйста,...
	Pukkuzheetyeh, puzharlooysta...
This is not what I'm _____ looking for	Это не то, что я ищу
	Eto nyeh tor, shtor ya eeshchoo
Thank you. I'll keep _____ looking	Спасибо. я поищу в другом месте
	Spasseeba. Ya puh-eeshchoo vdroogorm myestyeh
Do you have_____ something...?	Есть у вас что-нибудь...?
	Yest oo vuss shtor-niboot...?
– less expensive? _____	Есть у вас что-нибудь подешевле?
	Yest oo vuss shtor-niboot puddishevlyeh?

– something smaller? _____	**Есть у вас что-нибудь поменьше?** *Yest oo vuss shtor-niboot pummensha?*
– something larger? _____	**Есть у вас что-нибудь побольше?** *Yest oo vuss shtor-niboot pubborlsha?*
I'll take this one _____	**Это я возьму** *Eto ya vuzmoo*
Does it come with _____ instructions?	**Инструкция прилагается?** *Eenstrooktsiya preeluggahyetsa?*
It's too expensive _____	**Это слишком дорого** *Eto sleeshkum dorugga*
I'll give you... _____	**Я даю...** *Ya dayoo...*
Could you keep this for __ me? I'll come back for it later	**Отложите это, пожалуйста. я скоро вернусь** *Utluzheetyeh eto, puzharlooysta. Ya skora virnoos*
Have you got a bag _____ for me, please?	**Вы мне не дадите пакет?** *Vy mnyeh nyeh duddeetyeh pukkyet?*
Could you giftwrap _____ it, please?	**Вы можете это красиво упаковать?** *Vy morzhityeh eto krusseeva oopukkuvart?*

10.2 Food

I'd like a hundred _____ grams of..., please	**Сто грамм..., пожалуйста** *Stor grahm..., puzharlooysta*
– five hundred grams/ ___ half a kilo of...	**Полкило..., пожалуйста** *Polkeelor..., puzharlooysta*
– a kilo of... _____	**Килограмм..., пожалуйста** *Keelugrarm..., puzharlooysta*
Could you...it for me, _____ please?	**..., пожалуйста** *..., puzharlooysta*
Could you slice it/ _____ dice it for me, please?	**Порежьте на ломтики/куски, пожалуйста** *Purrayzhtyeh nah lormteeki/kooskee, puzharlooysta*

Can I order it? _____	Можно это заказать?
	Morzhna eta zukkuzzart?
I'll pick it up tomorrow/ __ at...	Я заберу это завтра в...часов
	Ya zubbiroo eto zarftra v...chussorf
Can you eat/drink this? __	Это можно есть/пить?
	Eto morzhna yest/peet?
What's in it? _____	Из чего это?
	Eess chivvor eta?

10.3 Clothing and shoes

I saw something in the___ window. Shall I point it out?	Я увидел(а) кое-что на витрине. Давайте покажу
	Ya ooveedyel(a) koyeh-shto nah veetreenyeh. Duvvigh-tyeh pukkuzhoo
I'd like something to_____ go with this	Я хочу что-нибудь подходящее к этому
	Ya khuchoo shtor-niboot puddkhudyashcheyeh ketummoo
Do you have shoes_____ to match this?	У вас есть туфли такого же цвета?
	Oo vuss yest toofli tukkorva zheh tsvyeta?
I'm a size...in European __ terms	Мой размер...по европейской системе
	Moy ruzzmyer...puh yevruppyayski seestyaymyeh
Can I try this on? _____	Можно померить?
	Morzhna pummyayreet?
Where's the fitting room?	Где примерочная?
	Gdyeh primyairuchnaya?
This is the right size _____	Это мой размер
	Eto moy ruzzmyer
It doesn't suit me _____	Мне не идёт
	Mnyeh nyeh eedyot
Do you have this/_____ these in...?	У вас это есть в...?
	Oo vuss eto yest v...?
The heel's too high/low __	Каблук слишком высокий/низкий
	Kublook sleeshkum vysorki/neeski

Is this/are these_____ genuine leather?	Это настоящая кожа? *Eto nastuyahshchaya korzha?*
I'm looking for a..._____ for a...-year-old baby/child	Я ищу...для ребёнка...лет *Ya eeshchoo...dlya ribyonka...lyet*
I'd like it in..._____	Я бы хотел(а)...из *Ya by khuttyel(a)....eess*
– silk _____	Я бы хотел(а)...из шёлка *Ya by khuttyel(a)... eess sholka*
– cotton_____	Я бы хотел(а)...из хлопка *Ya by khuttyel(a)....eess khlorpka*
– wool _____	Я бы хотел(а)...из шерсти *Ya by khuttyel(a)....eess shairsti*
– linen _____	Я бы хотел(а)...из льна *Ya by khuttyel(a)....eess lnah*
What temperature_____ can I wash it at?	При какой температуре можно это стирать? *Pree kukkoy tyemperatooryeh morzhna eto steerart?*
Will it shrink in the _____ wash?	Это садится при стирке? *Eto suddeetsa pree steerkyeh?*

Не гладить Do not iron	**Повесить в намоченном виде** Drip dry	**Ручная стирка** Hand wash
Не выжимать в центрифуге Do not spin dry	**Химчистка** Dry clean	**Машинная стирка** Machine wash

At the cobbler's

Could you mend _____ these shoes?	**Вы можете починить эти туфли?** *Vy morzhityeh puchinneet eti tooflee?*
Could you put new _____ soles/heels on these?	**Вы можете поставить новые подмётки/каблуки?** *Vy morzhityeh pustarvit norvy-yeh pudmyotki/kubblookee?*
When will they be _____ ready?	**Когда они будут готовы?** *Kugdah unnee boodoot guttorvy?*
I'd like..., please _____	**..., пожалуйста** *..., puzharlooysta*
– a tin of shoe polish _____	**Банку гуталина, пожалуйста** *Barnkoo gootulleena, puzharlooysta*
– a pair of shoelaces _____	**Шнурки, пожалуйста** *Shnoorkee, puzharlooysta*

10.4 Photographs and video

I'd like a film for this _____ camera, please	**Плёнку для этого фотоаппарата, пожалуйста** *Plyonkoo dlya etuvva futta-appurrarta, puzharlooysta*
– a cartridge _____	**Кассету, пожалуйста** *Kussyetoo, puzharlooysta*
– a one twenty-six _____ cartridge	**Кассету "сто двадцать шесть", пожалуйста** *Kussyetoo "stor dvartsut shest", puzharlooysta*
– a slide film _____	**Плёнку для слайдов, пожалуйста** *Plyonkoo dlya sligh-duff, puzharlooysta*
– a videotape _____	**Видеокассету, пожалуйста** *Veediokussyetoo, puzharlooysta*
colour/black and white __	**Цветная/чёрно-белая** *Tsvitnahya/chorna-byelaya*

super eight _____	**Супер восьмимиллиметровая лента** *Soopyer vussmeemeeleemitrorvaya lyenta*
12/24/36 exposures _____	**Двенадцать/двадцать четыре/тридцать шесть кадров** *Dvinartsut/dvartsut chityri/treetsut shest kardruff*
daylight film _____	**Плёнка для съёмки при дневном свете** *Plyonka dlya s-yomki pree dnivnorm svyetyeh*
film for artificial light _____	**Плёнка для съёмки при искусственном свете** *Plyonka dlya s-yomki pree eeskoostvinnum svyetyeh*

Problems

Could you load the _____ film for me, please?	**Вы можете зарядить фотоаппарат?** *Vy morzhityeh zurryuddeet futta-appurrart?*
Could you take the film __ out for me, please?	**Вы можете вынуть плёнку из фотоаппарата?** *Vy morzhityeh vynoot plyonkoo eess futta-appurrarta?*
Should I replace _____ the batteries?	**Нужно заменить батарейки?** *Noozhna zumineet baturrayki?*
Could you have a look ____ at my camera, please? It's not working	**Посмотрите, пожалуйста, мой фотоаппарат. Он не работает** *Pusmuttreetyeh, puzharlooysta, moy futta-appurrart. Orn nyeh rabortayet*
The...is broken_____	**...сломан(а)** *...slormun(a)*
The film's jammed_____	**Плёнку заело** *Plyonkoo zayelo*
The film's broken_____	**Плёнка порвалась** *Plyonka puhrvullars*
The flash isn't working ___	**Вспышка не работает** *Fspyshka nyeh rabortayet*

Processing and prints

I'd like to have this film __ developed/printed, please	Проявите/отпечатайте эту плёнку, пожалуйста *Prayaveetyeh/utpichartightyeh etoo plyonkoo, puzharlooysta*
I'd like...prints from_____ each negative	...отпечатков с каждого кадра, пожалуйста *...utpichartkoff s karzhduvva kardra, puzharlooysta*
glossy/matt _____	Глянцевый/матовый *Glyantsevy/martuvvy*
6x9_____	Шесть на девять *Shest na dyevit*
I'd like to re-order _____ these photos	Я хочу дополнительно заказать эти фотографии *Ya khuchoo duppulneetyelno zukkuzzart etee futtugrarfii*
I'd like to have this _____ photo enlarged	Мне нужно увеличить эту фотографию *Mnyeh noozhno ooveleechit etoo futtugrarfiyu*
How much is _____ processing?	Сколько стоит проявить? *Skorlka stor-eet pruh-yuvveet?*
– printing_____	Сколько стоит отпечатка? *Skorlka stor-eet utpechartka?*
– it to re-order _____	Сколько стоит дополнительный заказ? *Skorlka stor-eet duppulneetyelny zukkarss?*
– the enlargement _____	Сколько стоит увеличение? *Skorlka stor-eet oovillichayniye?*
When will they _____ be ready?	Когда они будут готовы? *Kugdar unnee boodoot guttorvy?*

10.5 At the hairdresser's

Do I have to make an ___ appointment?	**Нужно договориться заранее?** *Noozhna dugguvvurreetsa zurrarnye-yeh?*
Can I come in straight ___ away?	**Вы можете меня сейчас постричь?** *Vy morzhityeh minya say-charss pustreech?*
How long will I have ___ to wait?	**Сколько мне ждать?** *Skorlka mnyeh zhdart?*
I'd like a shampoo/ ___ haircut	**Я хочу помыть голову/я хочу постричься** *Ya khuchoo pummyt gorluvvoo/ya khuchoo pustreechsa*
I'd like a shampoo for ___ oily/dry hair, please	**Пожалуйста, шампунь для жирных/сухих волос** *Puzharlooysta, shumpoon dlya zheernykh/sookheekh vullorss*
– an anti-dandruff ___ shampoo	**Пожалуйста, шампунь против перхоти** *Puzharlooysta, shumpoon prorteeff pyairkhutti*
– a shampoo for ___ permed/coloured hair	**Пожалуйста, шампунь для химической завивки/крашеных волос** *Puzharlooysta, shumpoon dlya kheemeecheskoy zuvveefki/krarshunykh vullorss*
– a colour rinse shampoo	**Пожалуйста, красящий шампунь** *Puzharlooysta, krarsyashchi shumpoon*
– a shampoo with ___ conditioner	**Пожалуйста, шампунь с ополаскивателем** *Puzharlooysta, shumpoon suppullarskivuttyelyem*
Do you have a colour ___ chart, please?	**У вас есть гамма цветов?** *Oo vuss yest garma tsvitorff?*
I want to keep it the ___ same colour	**Такой же цвет, как сейчас** *Tukkoy zheh tsvyet, kukk saycharss*
I'd like it darker/lighter ___	**Я хочу темнее/светлее** *Ya khuchoo timnyay-yeh/svitlyay-yeh*

I'd like/I don't want _____ hairspray	**С укрепителем, пожалуйста (без укрепителя, пожалуйста)**
	Sookripp**ee**tyelyem, puzh**ar**looysta (byes ookkripp**ee**tyelya, puzh**ar**looysta)
– gel_____	**Гель, пожалуйста**
	Gyel, puzh**ar**looysta
– lotion _____	**Лосьон, пожалуйста**
	Luss-**yon**, puzh**ar**looysta
I'd like a short fringe_____	**Короткую чёлку, пожалуйста**
	Kurr**ort**kooyoo **chol**koo, puzh**ar**looysta
Not too short at the _____ back	**Сзади не очень коротко, пожалуйста**
	S-z**ar**di nyeh **or**chin korutka, puzh**ar**looysta
Not too long here _____	**Здесь покороче, пожалуйста**
	Zdyess pukkur**or**cheh, puzh**ar**looysta
I'd like/I don't want_____ (many) curls	**Завивку, пожалуйста (поменьше кудрей, пожалуйста)**
	Zuvv**ee**fku, puzh**ar**looysta (pumm**yen**sheh koodr**ay**, puzh**ar**looysta)
It needs a little/ _____ a lot taken off	**Отрежьте поменьше/побольше, пожалуйста**
	Utr**ay**zhtyeh pumm**yen**sheh/pubb**or**lsheh, puzh**ar**looysta

Как вас постричь?	How do you want it cut?
Какую бы вы хотели причёску?	What style did you have in mind?
Какой сделать цвет?	What colour did you want it?
Температура нормальная?	Is the temperature all right for you?
Хотите что-нибудь почитать?	Would you like something to read?
Хотите что-нибудь пить?	Would you like a drink?
Вас всё устраивает?	Is this what you had in mind?

want a completely _____ different style	Я хочу совсем другую причёску *Ya khuchoo suvsyem droogooyu preechosku*
I'd like it the same... _____	Я хочу причёску как... *Ya khuchoo preechosku kukk...*
– as that lady's _____	Я хочу причёску как у этой женщины *Ya khuchoo preechosku kukk oo etoy zhenshchiny*
– as in this photo _____	Я хочу причёску как на этой фотографии *Ya khuchoo preechosku kukk nah etoy futtugrarfii*
Could you put the_____ drier up/down a bit?	Поставьте, пожалуйста, колпак повыше/пониже *Pustarvtyeh, puzharlooysta, kullpark puvysha/punneezha*
I'd like a facial _____	Маску для лица, пожалуйста *Marskoo dlya leetsah, puzharlooysta*
– a manicure _____	Маникюр, пожалуйста *Munnikyoor, puzharlooysta*
– a massage_____	Массаж, пожалуйста *Massarsh, puzharlooysta*
Could you trim_____ my fringe?	Подстригите мне чёлку, пожалуйста *Puttstreegeetyeh mnyeh cholkoo, puzharlooysta*
– my beard? _____	Подстригите мне бороду, пожалуйста *Puttstreegeetyeh mnyeh boruddoo, puzharlooysta*
– my moustache? _____	Подровняйте мне усы, пожалуйста *Puddruvvnyightyeh mnyeh oosy, puzharlooysta*
I'd like a shave, please __	Побрейте, пожалуйста *Pubbraytyeh, puzharlooysta*
I'd like a wet shave, _____ please	Побрейте меня лезвием, пожалуйста *Pubbraytyeh minya lyayzveeyum, puzharlooysta*

127

11

At the Tourist Information Centre

11.1 Places of interest 129

11.2 Going out 131

11.3 Booking tickets 133

11.1 Places of interest

Where's the Tourist _____ Information Centre, please?	**Где туристическое бюро?** *Gdyeh tooreesteechiskoyeh byooror?*
Do you have a city map?_	**У вас есть план города?** *Oo vuss **yest** plarn gorrudda?*
Could you give me _____ some information about...?	**У вас есть информация о...?** *Oo vuss **yest** eenformartsiya or...?*
How much is that? _____	**Сколько с нас?** *Skorlka snarss?*
What are the main_____ places of interest?	**Какие самые известные достопримечательности?** *Kukkeeyeh sarmy-yeh eezvyestny-yeh dustuppreemichartyelnusti?*
Could you point them ___ out on the map?	**Покажите, пожалуйста, на карте** *Pukkuzheetyeh, puzharlooysta, nah kartyeh*
What do you _____ recommend?	**Что вы нам рекомендуете?** *Shtor vy narm rekummendooyetyeh?*
We'll be here for a_____ few hours	**Мы пробудем здесь пару часов** *My prubboodyum zdyess paroo chussorf*
– a day _____	**Мы пробудем здесь день** *My prubboodyum zdyess dyen*
– a week _____	**Мы пробудем здесь неделю** *My prubboodyum zdyess nidyaylyu*
We're interested in..._____	**Нас интересует...** *Nuss eentyeressooyet...*
Is there a scenic walk_____ around the city?	**Мы можем пройтись по городу?** *My morzhum pruytees po goruddoo?*
How long does it take? __	**Сколько это займёт времени?** *Skorlka eto zigh-myot vraymini?*
Where does it start/end? _	**Где начало/конец?** *Gdyeh nucharlo/kunnyets?*
Are there any boat _____ cruises here?	**Здесь есть теплоходные экскурсии?** *Zdyess yest tipplukhordny-yeh ekskoorsii?*

Where can we board?	**Где посадка?**
	Gdyeh pussartka?
Are there any bus tours?	**Есть ли автобусные экскурсии?**
	Yest-lee ufftorboosny-yeh ekskoorsii?
Where do we get on?	**Где посадка?**
	Gdyeh pussartka?
Is there a guide who speaks English?	**Есть ли гид, говорящий по-английски?**
	Yest lee geet, guvvurryashchi pa-ungleeski?
What trips can we take around the area?	**Какие можно сделать вылазки в окрестности?**
	Kukkeeyeh morzhna zdyelat vylaski vukkryesnusti?
Are there any excursions?	**Есть ли экскурсии?**
	Yest lee ekskoorsii?
Where do they go to?	**Куда?**
	Koodar?
We'd like to go to...	**Мы хотим в...**
	My khutteem v...
How long is the trip?	**Сколько длится поездка?**
	Skorlka dleetsa puh-yestka?
How long do we stay in...?	**Сколько времени мы пробудем в...?**
	Skorlka vraymini my prubboodyem v...?
Are there any guided tours?	**Будут ли экскурсии?**
	Boodoot lee ekskoorsii?
How much free time will we have there?	**Сколько у нас будет свободного времени?**
	Skorlka oo narss boodyet svubbordnuvva vraymini?
We want to go hiking	**Мы хотим в поход**
	My khutteem fpukhort
Can we hire a guide?	**Можно нанять гида?**
	Morzha nunnyat geeda?
What time does... open/close?	**Когда открывается/закрывается...?**
	Kugdar utkryvahyetsa/zukkryvahyetsa...?
What days is...open/ closed?	**По каким дням...открыт/закрыт?**
	Puh kakeem dnyam...utkryt/zukkryt?

What's the admission price?	Сколько стоит билет?
	Skorlka stor-eet beelyet?
Is there a group discount?	Есть ли скидка для групп?
	Yest-lee skeetka dlya groop?
Is there a child discount?	Есть ли скидка для детей?
	Yest-lee skeetka dlya dyityay?
Is there a discount for pensioners?	Есть ли скидка для пенсионеров?
	Yest-lee skeetka dlya pinsiunnyairoff?
Can I take (flash) photos	Здесь можно фотографировать (со вспышкой)/снимать?
	Zdyess morzhna futtagruffeerovart (suh fspyshkoy)/sneemart?
Do you have any postcards of...?	У вас есть открытки с...?
	Oo vuss yest utkrytki s...?
Do you have an English...?	У вас есть...на английском?
	Oo vuss yest...nah ungleeskum?
- an English catalogue?	У вас есть каталог на английском?
	Oo vuss yest kuttullork nah ungleeskum?
- an English programme?	У вас есть программа на английском?
	Oo vuss yest prugrarma nah ungleeskum?
- an English brochure?	У вас есть брошюра на английском?
	Oo vuss yest brushoora nah ungleeskum?

11.2 Going out

● **Tickets for theatres,** opera houses and concert halls can be bought for roubles from their ticket office or from stalls in public places, or for foreign currency through hotels and tourist agencies. Most foreign films are dubbed into Russian.

What's on tonight?	Куда сегодня можно пойти?
	Koodar sivordnya morzhna puytee?
We want to go to...	Мы хотим в...
	My khutteem v...
Which films are showing?	Какие идут фильмы?
	Kukkeeyeh eedoot feelmy?

What sort of film is that? _	**Что это за фильм?**
	***Shtor** e**to zah feelm?*
Suitable for the whole ___ family	**Все возрасты**
	*Fsyeh v**o**rzrusti*
Not suitable for children _ under twelve/sixteen years	**Детям до двенадцати/шестнадцати вход воспрещён**
	*Dy**e**tyum duh dvin**a**rtsuti/shistn**a**rtsuti fkhort vusprish**ch**on*
original version _____	**Недублированный**
	*Nyed**oob**l**ee**ruvv**a**nny*
subtitled _____	**С субтитрами**
	*S-soopt**ee**trami*
dubbed _____	**Дублированный**
	*D**oob**l**ee**ruvv**a**nny*
Is it a continuous_____ showing?	**Без антракта?**
	*Byes untr**a**rkta?*
What's on at...? _____	**Что можно посмотреть в...?**
	***Shtor** m**o**rzhna pussmutr**a**yt v...?*
– the theatre?_____	**Что можно посмотреть в театре?**
	***Shtor** m**o**rzhna pussmutr**a**yt fty**ea**rtreh?*
– the concert hall? _____	**Что можно послушать в концертном зале?**
	***Shtor** m**o**rzhna pusl**oo**shat fkunts**air**tnum z**a**rlyeh?*
– the opera?_____	**Что можно послушать в опере?**
	***Shtor** m**o**rzhna pusl**oo**shat v**o**rpyeryeh?*
Where can I find a good _ disco around here?	**Где здесь хорошая дискотека?**
	***Gdyeh** zdyess khurr**o**rshaya deeskuty**e**ka?*
Is it members only? _____	**Нужно быть членом?**
	*N**oo**zhna byt chly**e**num?*
Where can I find a good _ nightclub around here?	**Где здесь хороший ночной клуб?**
	***Gdyeh** zdyess khurr**o**rshiy nuchn**oy** kloop?*
Is it evening wear only? __	**Вечерняя одежда обязательна?**
	*Vich**air**naya udd**y**ezhda ubbyiz**a**rtyelna?*
Should I/we dress up? ___	**Вечерняя одежда желательна?**
	*Vich**air**naya udd**y**ezhda zhil**a**rtyelna?*

What time does the _____ show start?	**Во сколько начинается представление?**
	Vuh skorlka nuchinahyetsa pridstuvvlyayniye?
When's the next soccer __ match?	**Когда следующий футбольный матч?**
	Kudgah slyaydooyushchi footborlny mahch?
Who's playing? _____	**Кто играет?**
	Ktor eegrahyet?

11.3 Booking tickets

Could you book some _____ tickets for us?	**Вы можете для нас заказать?**
	Vy morzhitye dlya nuss zukkuzzart?
We'd like to book..._____ seats/a table...	**Мы хотим...мест/столик**
	My khutteem...myest/storlik
– in the stalls _____	**Мы хотим...мест/столик в зале**
	My khutteem...myest/storlik vzarlyeh
– on the balcony _____	**Мы хотим...мест/столик на балконе**
	My khutteem...myest/storlik nah bulkornyeh
– box seats_____	**Мы хотим...мест/столик в ложе**
	My khutteem...myest/storlik vlorzheh
– a table at the front_____	**Мы хотим...мест/столик спереди**
	My khutteem...myest/storlik spayridi
– in the middle_____	**Мы хотим...мест/столик посередине**
	My khutteem...myest/storlik pussireedeenyeh
– at the back _____	**Мы хотим...мест/столик сзади**
	My khutteem...myest/storlik s-zardi
Could I book...seats for __ the...o'clock performance?	**Можно заказать...мест на представление в...часов?**
	Morzhna zukkuzzart...myest nah pridstuvvlyayniye v...chussorf?
Are there any seats left __ for tonight?	**Есть ещё билеты на вечер?**
	***Yest** yishchor beelyety nah **vay**chir?*

How much is a ticket? ___	**Сколько стоит билет?**
	Skorlka stor-eet beelyet?
When can I pick the _____ tickets up?	**Когда я могу забрать билеты?**
	Kugdar ya muggoo zubbrart beelyety?
I've got a reservation _____	**Я заказывал(а)**
	Ya zukkarzyval(a)
My name's..._____	**Моя фамилия...**
	Muyah fameeliya

На какое представление вы хотите заказать?	Which performance do you want to book for?
Где вы хотите сидеть?	Where would you like to sit?
Все билеты распроданы	Everything's sold out
Только стоячие места	It's standing room only
Только места на балконе	We've only got balcony seats left
Только места на галёрке	We've only got seats left in the gallery
Только места в зале	We've only got stalls seats left
Только места спереди	We've only got seats left at the front
Только места сзади	We've only got seats left at the back
Сколько мест?	How many seats would you like?
Вы должны забрать билеты до ... часов	You'll have to pick up the tickets before...o'clock
Ваши билеты, пожалуйста	Tickets, please
Вот ваше место	This is your seat

12.1 Sporting questions 136

12.2 By the waterfront 136

12.3 In the snow 138

12.1 Sporting questions

Where can we... _____ around here?	**Где мы можем...?** *Gdyeh my morzhum...?*
Is there a... _____ around here?	**Здесь есть...поблизости?** *Zdyess yest...publeezusti?*
Can I hire a...here? _____	**Здесь можно взять напрокат...?** *Zdyess morzhna vzyaht nupprukkart...?*
Can I take...lessons? ____	**Можно брать уроки...?** *Morzhna brat oororki...?*
How much is that per____ hour/per day/a turn?	**Сколько это стоит в день/в час/за один раз?** *Skorlka eto stor-eet vdyen/fcharss/zah uddeen rahss?*
Do I need a permit _____ for that?	**Нужно ли для этого разрешение?** *Noozhna lee dlya etuvva ruzrishayniyeh?*
Where can I get_____ the permit?	**Где можно получить разрешение?** *Gdyeh morzhna puloocheet ruzrishayniye?*

12.2 By the waterfront

Is it a long way to _____ the sea still?	**Ещё далеко до моря?** *Yishchor dullikor duh morya?*
Is there a...around here? _	**Здесь есть поблизости также...?** *Zdyess yest pubbleezusti tarkzheh...?*
– an outdoor/indoor/ ____ public swimming pool	**Здесь есть поблизости также бассейн?** *Zdyess yest pubbleezusti tarkzheh bussayn?*
– a sandy beach _____	**Здесь есть поблизости также песочный пляж?** *Zdyess yest pubbleezusti tarkzheh pissorchny plyarsh?*

– a nudist beach _____	**Здесь есть поблизости также пляж нудистов?** *Zdyess **yest** pubbl**ee**zusti t**ar**kzheh plyarsh nood**ee**stuff?*
– mooring _____	**Здесь есть поблизости также пристань для лодок?** *Zdyess **yest** pubbl**ee**zusti t**ar**kzheh pr**ee**estun dlya l**or**duk?*
Are there any rocks_____ here?	**Здесь есть скалы?** *Zdyess **yest** sk**ar**ly?*
When's high/low tide? ___	**Когда прилив/отлив?** *Kugd**ar** preel**ee**f/utl**ee**f?*
What's the water _____ temperature?	**Какова температура воды?** *Kukkuvv**ar** tyemperat**oo**ra vudd**y**?*
Is it (very) deep here?____	**Здесь (очень) глубоко?** *Zdyess (**or**chin) gloobukk**or**?*
Can you stand here? ____	**Здесь можно стоять?** *Zdyess m**or**zhna stuh**yart**?*
Is it safe (for children)_____ to swim here?	**Здесь безопасно (для детей)?** *Zdyess byezupp**ar**ssno (dlya dyit**yay**)?*
Are there any currents? __	**Есть ли течение?** *Yest-lee tich**ay**niye?*
Are there any rapids/ _____ waterfalls in this river?	**На этой реке есть стремнины/водопады?** *Nah **e**toy rikk**yeh** yest purr**or**gi/vuddup**ar**dy?*
What does that flag/_____ buoy mean?	**Что означает этот флаг/буй?** ***Shtor** uznuch**ah**yet **e**tut flahk/booy?*

Запрещено повить рыбу No fishing	**Только с разрешением** Permits only	**Запрещено заниматься серфингом** No surfing
Место для рыбной ловли Fishing water	**Запрещено купаться** No swimming	**Опасно!** Danger

Is there a lifeguard on duty here?	**Здесь есть спасательная служба, которая за всем присматривает?** *Zdyess yest spussartyelnaay sloozhba, kuttoraya za fsyem preesmartrivayaet?*
Are dogs allowed here?	**Собакам сюда можно?** *Subbarkum syoodar morzhna?*
Is camping on the beach allowed?	**Можно поставить палатку на пляже?** *Morzhna pustarvit pullartkoo nah plyarzheh?*
Are we allowed to build a fire here?	**Можно здесь разжечь костёр?** *Morzhna zdyess ruz-zhaych kustyor?*

12.3 In the snow

Can I take ski lessons here?	**Здесь можно взять уроки по катанию на (горных) лыжах?** *Zdyess morzhna vzyart oororki puh kuttarneeyu nah (gornykh) lyzhakh?*
for beginners/advanced	**Для начинающих/(полу)продвинутых** *Dlya nuchinahyooshchikh/ (pulloo-)prudveenootykh*
How large are the groups?	**Сколько человек в группах?** *Skorlka chiluvvyek vgroopukh?*
What language are the classes in?	**На каком языке уроки?** *Nah kukkorm yazykyeh oororki?*
Must I give you a passport photo?	**Нужна ли фотография для пропуска?** *Noozhnar lee futtagrarfiya dlya prorpuska?*
Where can I have a passport photo taken?	**Где можно сфотографироваться?** *Gdyeh morzhna sfuttagraffeerovartsa?*
Are there any runs for cross-country skiing?	**Есть ли поблизости лыжные трассы?** *Yest-lee pubbleezusti lyzhny-yeh trarssy?*
Have the cross-country runs been marked?	**Лыжные трассы указаны?** *Lyzhny-yeh trarssy ookarzunny?*

13.1 Call (fetch) the doctor 140

13.2 Patient's ailments 140

13.3 The consultation 142

13.4 Medication and prescriptions 146

13.5 At the dentist's 147

13.1 Call (fetch) the doctor

Could you call/fetch a ____ doctor quickly, please?	**Вызовите/найдите скорее врача, пожалуйста**
	Vyzzuvveetyeh/nigh-deetyeh skurray-yeh vruchah, puzharlooysta
When does the doctor ____ have surgery?	**Когда у врача приём?**
	Kugdar oo vruchah preeyom?
When can the doctor ____ come?	**Когда врач может прийти?**
	Kugdar vrarch morzhit preetee?
I'd like to make an _____ appointment to see the doctor	**Назначьте для меня приём у врача, пожалуйста**
	Nazznarchtyeh dlya minya preeyom oo vruchah, puzharlooysta
I've got an appointment__ to see the doctor at...	**Мне к врачу к...часам**
	Mnyeh kvruchoo k...chussarm
Which doctor/chemist ____ has night/weekend duty?	**Какой врач/какая аптека работает ночью/в выходные?**
	Kukkoy vrarch/kukkahya uptyeka rubbortayet norchyu/v vykhudny-yeh?

13.2 Patient's ailments

I don't feel well _____	**Я себя плохо чувствую**
	Ya sibya plorkha choostvooyu
I'm dizzy _____	**У меня кружится голова**
	Oo minya kroozhitsa gulluvar
– ill _____	**Я болен (больна)**
	Ya borlyen (bulnar)
– sick _____	**Меня тошнит**
	Minya tushneet
I've got a cold _____	**Я простудился (простудилась)**
	Ya prustoodeelsa (prustoodeelas)

It hurts here _____	**У меня здесь болит**
	Oo minya zdyess bulleet
I've been throwing up ___	**Меня стошнило**
	Minya stushneela
I've got..._____	**У меня болит...**
	Oo minya bulleet...
I'm running a _____ temperature of...degrees.	**У меня температура...градусов**
	Oo minya tyemperatoora...grardoosuff
I've been stung by _____ a wasp	**Меня укусила оса**
	Minya ookooseela ussar
I've been stung by an____ insect	**Меня укусило насекомое**
	Minya ookooseela nassikormoyeh
I've been bitten by _____ a dog	**Меня укусила собака**
	Minya ookooseela subbarka
I've been stung by _____ a jellyfish	**Меня ужалила медуза**
	Minya oozharleela midooza
I've been bitten by _____ a snake	**Меня ужалила змея**
	Minya oozharleela zmiyah
I've been bitten by _____ an animal	**Меня укусил зверь**
	Minya ookooseel zvyair
I've cut myself _____	**Я порезался (порезалась)**
	Ya puhryezalsya (puhryezalas)
I've burned myself _____	**Я обжёгся (обожглась)**
	Ya ubzhoksa (ubuzhglarss)
I've grazed myself_____	**Я ободрал (ободрала)...**
	Ya ubbudrarl (ubbudrullar)...
I've had a fall _____	**Я упал(а)**
	Ya ooparl(a)
I've sprained my ankle ___	**Я вывихнул(а) щиколотку**
	Ya vyvikhnool(a) shchikullortkoo

13.3 The consultation

На что жалуетесь?	What seems to be the problem?
Как долго вы на это жалуетесь?	How long have you had these symptoms?
У вас уже было подобное раньше?	Have you had this trouble before?
Какая у вас температура?	How high is your temperature?
Разденьтесь, пожалуйста	Get undressed, please
Разденьтесь до пояса, пожалуйста	Strip to the waist, please
Вы можете там раздеться	You can undress there
Обнажите левую/правую руку, пожалуйста	Roll up your left/right sleeve, please
Лягте здесь, пожалуйста	Lie down here, please
Больно?	Does this hurt?
Дышите глубоко	Breathe deeply
Откройте рот	Open your mouth

Patient's medical history

I'm a diabetic _____	У меня диабет
	Oo minya diabyet
I have a heart condition __	У меня больное сердце
	Oo minya bullnor-yeh sairtseh
I have asthma _____	У меня астма
	Oo minya arstma
I'm allergic to... _____	У меня аллергия на...
	Oo minya ullairgeeya nah...
I'm...months pregnant ___	Я на...месяце беременности
	Ya nah...myaysyutseh biryayminusti

У вас есть аллергия на что-нибудь?	Do you have any allergies?
Принимаете лекарства?	Are you on any medication?
Вы на диете?	Are you on a diet?
Вы беременны?	Are you pregnant?
Вам делали прививку от столбняка?	Have you had a tetanus injection?

I'm on a diet_____	**Я на диете**
	*Ya nah dee**yet**yeh*
I'm on medication/the pill	**Я принимаю лекарства/ противозачаточные таблетки**
	*Ya preeneem**ah**yu lik**ar**stva/ pruteevazuch**ar**tuchny-yeh tubl**yet**ki*
I've had a heart attack ___ once before	**У меня уже был раньше приступ сердца**
	*Oo minya ooz**heh** byl **rar**nsheh pr**ee**stoop **sair**tsa*
I've had a(n)...operation __	**У меня была операция на...**
	*Oo minya byl**ar** uppir**ar**tsiya nah...*
I've been ill recently _____	**Я только что переболел(а)**
	*Ya **tor**lka shtor pirribull**yel**(a)*
I've got an ulcer _____	**У меня язва желудка**
	*Oo minya **yar**zva zhill**oo**tka*
I've got my period_____	**У меня менструация**
	*Oo minya menstroo**ar**tsiya*

Ничего серьёзного	It's nothing serious
Вы сломали...	Your...is broken
Вы ушибли...	You've got a/some bruised...
Вы порвали...	You've got (a) torn...
У вас воспаление	You've got an inflammation
У вас аппендицит	You've got appendicitis
У вас бронхит	You've got bronchitis
У вас венерическая болезнь	You've got a venereal disease
У вас грипп	You've got the flu
У вас был сердечный приступ	You've had a heart attack
У вас (вирусная, бактериологическая) инфекция	You've got an infection (viral, bacterial)
У вас воспаление лёгких	You've got pneumonia
У вас язва желудка	You've got an ulcer
Вы растянули мышцу	You've pulled a muscle
У вас инфекция во влагалище	You've got a vaginal infection
У вас пищевое отравление	You've got food poisoning
У вас солнечный удар	You've got sunstroke
У вас аллергия на ...	You're allergic to...
Вы беременны	You're pregnant
Я хочу исследовать вашу кровь/мочу/кал	I'd like to have your blood/urine/stools tested
Необходимо зашить	It needs stitching
Я вас направляю к специалисту/в больницу	I'm referring you to a specialist/sending you to hospital
Нужно сделать снимки	You'll need to have some x-rays taken
Подождите, пожалуйста, в приёмнойroom,	Could you wait in the waiting room, please?
Необходима операция	You'll need an operation

The diagnosis

Is it contagious? _____	**Это заразно?**
	Eto zurrarzna?
How long do I have to ___ stay...?	**Сколько мне придётся пробыть...?**
	Skorlka mnyeh preedyotsa prubbyt...?
– in bed_____	**Сколько мне придётся пробыть в постели?**
	Skorlka mnyeh preedyotsa prubbyt fpustyayli?
– in hospital _____	**Сколько мне придётся пробыть в больнице?**
	Skorlka mnyeh preedyotsa prubbyt vbulneetseh?
Do I have to go on _____ a special diet?	**Мне нужно сесть на диету?**
	Mnyeh noozhna syest na dee-etoo?
Am I allowed to travel? __	**Мне можно путешествовать?**
	Mnyeh morzhna pootyeshestvuvvart?
Can I make a new_____ appointment?	**Можно с вами договориться на следующий раз?**
	Morzhna svarmi dugguvvurreetsa na slyaydooyushchiy rahss?
When do I have to _____ come back?	**Когда мне снова прийти?**
	Kugdar mnyeh snorva preetee?
I'll come back _____ tomorrow	**Я приду завтра снова**
	Ya preedoo zarftra snorva

Вы должны снова прийти завтра/через ... дней	Come back tomorrow/in...days' time

13.4 Medication and prescriptions

How do I take this_____ medicine?	**Как принимать это лекарство?** *Kukk preeneemart eto likarstva?*
How many capsules/____ drops/injections/ spoonfuls/tablets each time?	**Сколько капсул/капель/уколов/ложек/ таблеток за раз?** *Skorlka karpsool/karpyel/ookorluff/ lorzhik/tubblyetuk zah rahss?*
How many times a day? _	**Сколько раз в день?** *Skorlka rahss vdyen?*
I've forgotten my_____ medication. At home I take...	**Я забыл(а) лекарства. Дома я принимаю...** *Ya zubbyl(a) likarstva. Dorma ya preeneemahyu...*
Could you make out a ____ prescription for me?	**Выпишите мне рецепт, пожалуйста** *Vypishyteh mnyeh ritsept, puzharlooysta*

в течение...дней for...days	**перед едой** before meals	**только для наружного употребления** not for internal use
завершить лечение to finish the course	**принимать** to take	
каждые...часов every...hours	**...раз в сутки...** times a day	**уколы** injections
капли drops	**растворить в воде** to dissolve in water	**целиком проглатывать** swallow whole
капсулы capsules	**столовые/чайные ложки** tablespoons/ teaspoons	**эти лекарства влияют на способность управлять машиной** this medication impairs your driving
мазать rub on		
мазь ointment	**таблетки** tablets	

я вам прописываю антибиотики/ микстуру/успокаивающее средство/ болеутоляющие средства	I'm prescribing antibiotics/a mixture/a tranquillizer/pain killers
Необходим покой	Have lots of rest
Вам нельзя выходить на улицу	Stay indoors
Вы должны оставаться в постели	Stay in bed

13.5 At the dentist's

Do you know a good _____ dentist?	**Вы не знаете хорошего зубного врача?** *Vy nyeh zna**h**yetye khurr**or**shivo zoobn**or**va vruch**ar**?*
Could you make a_____ dentist's appointment for me? It's urgent	**Запишите меня на приём к зубному врачу, пожалуйста. Мне нужно срочно.** *Zuppish**y**tyeh min**ya** nah pree**yom** k zoobn**or**moo vruch**oo**, puzh**ar**loo**y**sta. Mnyeh n**oo**zhna sr**or**chna.*
Can I come in today, _____ please?	**Мне можно прийти прямо сегодня?** *Mnyeh m**or**zhna preet**ee** pry**ar**ma siv**or**dnya?*
I have (terrible)_____ toothache	**У меня (ужасно) болит зуб** *Oo min**ya** oozh**ar**ssno bull**ee**t zoop*
Could you prescribe/ _____ give me a painkiller?	**Вы можете мне прописать/дать болеутоляющее?** *Vy m**or**zhityeh mnyeh prupp**ee**ss**art**/dart borlyeootull**yah**yooshchiyeh?*
A piece of my tooth _____ has broken off	**У меня отломился кусочек зуба** *Oo min**ya** utlumm**ee**lsya koos**or**chek z**oo**ba*

My filling's come out ____	**У меня выпала пломба**
	Oo minya vypala plormba.
I've got a broken crown __	**У меня сломалась коронка**
	Oo minya slummarlas kurrornka
I'd like/I don't want a ____ local anaesthetic	**Я хочу/не хочу местный наркоз**
	Ya khuchoo/nyeh khuchoo myestny narkorss
Can you do a makeshift__ repair job?	**Вы можете мне временно помочь?**
	Vy morzhityeh mnyeh vrayminna pummorch?
I don't want this tooth ____ pulled	**Не вырывайте этот зуб**
	Nyeh vyryvightyeh etut zoop
My dentures are broken. _ Can you fix them?	**У меня сломался протез. Вы можете его починить?**
	Oo minya slummarlsya pruttess. Vy morzhityeh yivvor puchineet?

Какой зуб болит?	Which tooth hurts?
У вас нарыв	You've got an abscess
Нужно обработать нерв	I'll have to do a root canal
Я сделаю местный наркоз	I'm giving you a local anaesthetic
Нужно этот зуб запломбировать вырвать/обточить	I'll have to fill/pull this tooth/file this...down
Нужно сверлить	I'll have to drill
Откройте рот	Open wide, please
Закройте рот	Close your mouth, please
Прополощите	Rinse, please
Всё ещё болит?	Does it hurt still?

14.1 Asking for help 150

14.2 Loss 151

14.3 Accidents 152

14.4 Theft 153

14.5 Missing person 153

14.6 The police 154

14.1 Asking for help

Help!	**Помогите!** *Pummugeetyeh!*
Fire!	**Пожар!** *Puzhar!*
Police!	**Милиция!** *Meeleetsiya!*
Quick!	**Быстро!** *Bystra!*
Danger!	**Опасно!** *Upparsna!*
Watch out!	**Осторожно!** *Usturrorzhna!*
Stop!	**Стоп!** *Storp!*
Be careful!	**Осторожно!** *Usturrorzhna!*
Don't!	**Не надо!** *Nyeh narda!*
Let go!	**Отпустите!** *Utpoosteetyeh!*
Stop that thief!	**Держи вора!** *Dyerzhee vora!*
Could you help me, please?	**Помогите, пожалуйста** *Pummuggeetyeh, puzharlooysta*
Where's the police station/emergency exit/fire escape?	**Где отделение милиции?/где запасной выход?/где пожарная лестница?** *Gdyeh utdilyayniyeh mileetsii?/gdyeh zuppussnoy vykhud?/gdyeh puzharnaya lyesnitsa?*
Where's the nearest fire extinguisher?	**Где огнетушитель?** *Gdyeh ugnyetoosheetyel?*
Call the fire brigade!	**Предупредите пожарную команду!** *Predoopriddeetyeh puzharnooyu kummarndoo!*

Call the police!	**Позвоните в милицию!**
	Puzvunneetyeh vmileetsiyu!
Call an ambulance!	**Вызовите скорую помощь!**
	Vyzuvveetyeh skorooyu pormushch!
Where's the nearest phone?	**Где телефон?**
	Gdyeh tyeliforn?
Could I use your phone?	**Можно позвонить по вашему телефону?**
	Morzhna puzvunneet puh varshimoo tyelifornoo?
What's the number for the police?	**Какой телефон вызова милиции?**
	Kukkoy tyeliforn vyzuvva mileetsii?

14.2 Loss

I've lost my purse/ wallet	**Я потерял(а) кошелёк/бумажник**
	Ya puttyiryarl(a) kushilyok/boomarzhnik
I lost my...yesterday	**Я вчера забыл(а) ...**
	Ya vchirar zubbyl(a) ...
I left my...here	**Я здесь оставил(а) ...**
	Ya zdyess ustarveel(a) ...
Did you find my...?	**Вы не находили ...?**
	Vy nyeh nukhuddeeli ...?
It was right here	**Он стоял/лежал здесь**
	Orn stuh-yarl/lyizharl zdyess
It's quite valuable	**Это очень ценная вещь**
	Eto orchin tsen-naya vyeshch
Where's the lost property office?	**Где бюро находок?**
	Gdyeh byooror nukhordukk?

14.3 Accidents

There's been an accident	**Произошёл несчастный случай** *Pruh-eezoshorl nischarstny sloochay*
Someone's fallen into _____ the water	**Человек упал в воду** *Chiluvvyek ooparl v vordoo*
There's a fire _____	**Пожар** *Puzhar*
Is anyone hurt? _____	**Кто-нибудь ранен?** *Ktor-neeboot rarnyun?*
Some people have _____ been/no one's been injured	**Есть пострадавшие (нет пострадавших)** *Yest pustruddarfsheeyeh (nyet pustruddarfshikh)*
There's someone in _____ the car/train still	**Ещё кто-то остался в машине/поезде** *Yishchor ktor-to ustarlsya vmushinyeh/ por-yizdyeh*
It's not too bad. Don't _____ worry	**Ничего страшного. Не беспокойтесь** *Nichivvor strarshnuvva. Nyeh byespukkoytyes*
Leave everything the _____ way it is, please	**Ничего не трогайте** *Nichivvor nyeh trorgightyeh*
I want to talk to the _____ police first	**Я хочу сначала поговорить с милицией** *Ya khuchoo snucharla pugguvvurreet smileetsiyay*
I want to take a _____ photo first	**Я хочу сначала сфотографировать** *Ya khuchoo snucharla sfuttagruffeerovat*
Here's my name _____ and address	**Вот моя фамилия и адрес** *Vort muh-yah fameeliya ee ardriss*
Could I have your _____ name and address?	**Можно вашу фамилию и адрес?** *Morzhna varshoo fameeliyu i ardriss?*
Could I see some _____ identification/your insurance papers?	**Можно ваше удостоверение личности?/Можно вашу страховку?** *Morzhna varsha oodustuvvviryayniyeh leechnusti? Morzhna varshoo strukhofkoo?*
Will you act as a _____ witness?	**Вы хотите быть свидетелем?** *Vy khutteetyeh byt sveedyaytyelyum?*

I need the details for ____ the insurance	Мне нужны данные для страховки *Mnyeh noozhny darn-ny-yeh dlya strukhofki*
Are you insured? _____	Вы застрахованы? *Vy zustrukhorvany?*
Could you sign here, ____ please?	Распишитесь здесь, пожалуйста *Rasspishytyes zdyess, puzharlooysta*

14.4 Theft

I've been robbed _____	Меня обокрали *Minya ubbukkrarli*
My...has been stolen ____	У меня украли... *Oo minya ookrarli...*
My car's been _____ broken into	Моя машина взломана *Muy-ya mushina vzlormunna*

14.5 Missing person

I've lost my child/ _____ grandmother	Я потерял(а) ребёнка/бабушку *Ya putyiryarl(a) ribyonka/barbooshku*
Could you help me _____ find him/her?	Вы мне поможете искать? *Vy mnyeh pummorzhityeh eeskart?*
Have you seen a _____ small child?	Вы не видели ребёнка? *Vy nyeh veedyeli ribyonka?*
He's/she's...years old ____	Ему/ей...лет *Yimoo/yay...lyet*
He's/she's got _____ short/long/blonde/red/ brown/black/grey/curly/ straight/frizzy hair	У него/неё короткие/длинные/светлые/ рыжие/каштановые/тёмные/седые/кудр явые/прямые/ вьющиеся волосы *Oo nyivvor/nyiyor kurrortkiyeh/dleeny- yeh/svyetly-yeh/ryzhiyeh/kushtarnuvy- yeh/tyomny-yeh/sidy-yeh/koodryarvy- yeh/pryummy-yeh/v-yooshchiyehsya vorlussy*

with a ponytail _____	**С хвостиком**
	Skhvorstikum
with plaits _____	**С косичками**
	Skusseechkummi
in a bun_____	**С пучком**
	Spoochkorm
He's/she's got _____ blue/brown/green eyes	**Глаза голубые/карие/зелёные**
	Gluzzah gullooby-yeh/kariyeh/zilyony-yeh
He's wearing swimming__ trunks/mountaineering boots	**На нём плавки/горные ботинки**
	Nah nyom plarfki/gorny-yeh butteenki
with/without glasses/ ____ a bag	**В очках/без очков, с сумкой/без сумки**
	Vuchkarkh/byez uchkorff, s-soomkoy/byes soomki
tall/short _____	**Большой (большая)/маленький (маленькая)**
	Bulshoy (bulshaya)/marlinki (marlinkaya)
This is a photo of _____ him/her	**Вот его/её фотография**
	Vort yivvor/yiyor futtagrarfiya
He/she must be lost_____	**Он/она, скорее всего, заблудился (заблудилась)**
	Orn/unnar, skurryay-yeh fsivvor, zubbloodeelsya (zubbloodeelas)

14.6 The police

An arrest

I don't speak Russian_____	**Я не говорю по-русски**
	Ya nyeh guvvurryoo puh-rooski
I didn't see the sign _____	**Я не видел(а) этого знака**
	Ya nyeh veedyel(a) etuvva znarka
I don't understand _____ what it says	**Я не понимаю, что там написано**
	Ya nyeh punnimahyu, shtor tarm nuppeesunna

Ваши документы на машину, пожалуйста	Your vehicle registration papers, please
Вы превысили скорость	You were speeding
Вы нарушили правила стоянки	You're not allowed to park here
У вас не работают фары	Your lights aren't working
С вас штраф...	You are fined...
Вы можете сразу заплатить?	Can you pay on the spot?
Вам нужно сразу заплатить	You must pay on the spot

I was only doing... kilometres an hour	Я ехал(а) всего...километров в час *Ya yekhal(a) fsivvor...keelummyetruff fcharss*
I'll have my car checked	Я отдам проверить машину *Ya utdarm pruvvyairit mushinoo*
I was blinded by oncoming lights	Меня ослепил встречный свет *Minya uslyepeel fstraychny svyet*

At the police station

I want to report a collision/a theft/rape	Я хочу сообщить об аварии/о потере/об изнасиловании *Ya khuchoo suh-ubshcheet ub avarii/o puttyairyeh/ub eeznusseeluvarnii*
Could you make out a report, please?	Составьте протокол, пожалуйста *Sustarvtyeh pruttukkorl, puzharlooysta*
Could I have a copy for the insurance?	Можно справку для страховки? *Morzhna sprarfkoo dlya strukhorfki?*
I've lost everything	Я всё потерял(а) *Ya fsyo puttyeryarl(a)*
My money has run out and I don't know what to do	У меня кончились деньги, я совершенно растерян(а) *Oo minya korncheelees dyengi, ya suvvirshenna rastyeryun(a)*

I'd like an interpreter ____	Мне нужен переводчик
	Mnyeh noozhun pirivortchik
I'm innocent ____	Я не виноват(а)
	Ya nyeh veenuvvart(a)
I don't know anything____ about it	Я ничего не знаю
	Ya nichivvor nyeh znahyu
I want to speak to____ someone from the British consulate	Я хочу поговорить с кем-нибудь из консульства Великобритании
	Ya khuchoo pugguvvurreet skyem-neeboot eess kornsoolstva Vileekobrittarnii
I need to see someone __ from the British embassy	Я хочу поговорить с кем-нибудь из посольства Великобритании
	Ya khuchoo pugguvvurreet skyem-neeboot eess pussorlstva Vileekobrittarnii
I want a lawyer who ____ speaks English	Мне нужен адвокат, который говорит по-английски/по
	Mnyeh noozhun udvukkart, kuttory guvvureet puh-ungleeski/puh

Где это случилось?	Where did it happen?
Что вы потеряли?	What's missing?
Что украдено?	What's been taken?
Можно ваше удостоверение личности?	Could I see some identification?
Когда это произошло?	What time did it happen?
Кто при этом присутствовал?	Who was involved?
Свидетели есть?	Are there any witnesses?
Заполните, пожалуйста	Fill this out, please
Подпишите здесь, пожалуйста	Sign here, please
Вам нужен переводчик?	Do you want an interpreter?

Word list English – Russian 158

Word list English – Russian

● **This word list** is intended to supplement the previous chapters. In a number of cases, words not included in this list can be found elsewhere in the book, for example alongside the diagrams of the car, the bicycle and the camping equipment. Many food words can be found in the Russian-English list in 4.7.

Abbreviations used: n=noun, vb=verb, adj=adjective, advb=adverb. With adjectives the masculine form is given, sometimes with the feminine in brackets.

A

above	наверху	*navirkhoo*
abroad	заграница	*zuggrunneetsa*
accident	несчастный случай	*nyehshcharstny sloochigh*
adder	гадюка	*guddyooka*
addition (maths)	сложение	*sluzhayniyeh*
address	адрес	**ard**riss
admission	вход	*fkhort*
admission price	входная плата	*fkhuddnahya plarta*
advice	совет	*suvvyet*
after	после	*porsslyeh*
afternoon	днём	*dnyom*
aftershave	одеколон после	*uddikullorn porslyeh*
	бритья	*breetyah*
again	снова	*snorva*
against	против	*prorteef*
age	возраст	*vorzrust*
Aids	СПИД	*SPEET*
air conditioning	кондиционер	*kundeetsionyair*
air mattress	надувной матрац	*nuddoovnoy muttrats*
air sickness bag	гигиенический	*geegeeyeneecheski*
	пакет	*pukkyet*
aircraft	самолёт	*summalyot*
airmail (by)	авиапочтой	*arviaporchtoy*
airport	аэропорт	*ah-airupport*

airport	аэропорт	*ah-airoport*
alarm	тревога	*trivorga*
alarm clock	будильник	*boodeelnik*
alcohol	алкоголь	*alkuggorl*
alcoholic drink	спиртной напиток	*speertnoy nuppeetuk*
all the time	постоянно	*pustuhyanno*
allergic	аллергический	*ullyergeecheski*
alone	один (одна)	*uddeen (uddnar)*
always	всегда	*fsigdar*
ambulance	скорая (помощь)	*skoraya (pormushch)*
amount	сумма	*soom-ma*
amusement park	парк отдыха	*park ortdykha (ee*
	(и развлечений)	*razvlichaynee)*
anaesthetize	обезболить	*ubbyuzborleet*
anchovy	анчоус	*unchor-oos*
and	и	*ee*
angry	сердитый	*syairdeety*
animal	животное	*zhivvortnoyeh*
ankle	лодыжка	*luddyshka*
answer	ответ	*utvyet*
ant	муравей	*mooruvvay*
antibiotics	антибиотик	*untibeeortik*
antifreeze	антифриз	*untifreess*
antique	античный	*unteechny*
antiques	антикварная вещь	*untikvarnaya vyeshch*
anus	задний проход	*zardni prukhort*
apartment	квартира	*kvarteera*
aperitif	аперитив	*uppyereeteef*
apologies	извинения	*eezvinyayniya*
apple	яблоко	*yarblukka*
apple juice	яблочный сок	*yarbluchny sork*
apple pie	пирог с яблоками	*peerork syarblukkummi*
apple sauce	яблочный мусс	*yarbluchny mooss*
appointment	приём	*preeyom*
approximately	приблизительно	*preebleezeetyelna*
apricot	абрикос	*ubbreekorss*
April	апрель	*upryel*

archbishop	архиепископ	*arkhiyepeeskup*
architecture	архитектура	*arkhityektoora*
area	окрестность	*ukryesnust*
arm	рука	*rookar*
arrange	договориться	*dugguvvureetsa*
arrive	прийти/приехать	*preetee/preeyekhat*
arrow	стрела	*strillar*
art	искусство	*eeskoostva*
artery	артерия	*artyayreeya*
artichokes	артишоки	*artishorki*
article	товар	*tuvvar*
artificial respiration	искусственное	*eeskoostven-noyeh*
	дыхание	*dykharniyeh*
arts and crafts	прикладное	*preekludnoryeh*
	искусство	*eeskoostva*
ashtray	пепельница	*pyaypilneetsa*
ask (for)	просить	*prusseet*
ask (question)	спросить	*sprusseet*
asparagus	спаржа	*sparzha*
aspirin	аспирин	*aspeereen*
assault	попытка к	*puppytka*
	изнасилованию	*keeznussee luvvarniyu*
at once	сразу	*srarzoo*
at the front	впереди	*fpiridee*
at the latest	не позже	*nyeh porzheh*
aubergine	баклажан	*bukkluzharn*
August	август	*arvgoost*
automatic	автоматический	*ufftummutteecheski*
autumn	осень	*orsin*
avalanche	лавина	*luveena*
awake	проснувшись	*prusnoofshees*
awning	ширма от солнца	*sheerma u sorntsa*
axe	топор	*tupporr*

baby	ребёнок	*ribyonuk*
baby food	детское питание	*dyetskoyeh peetarniyeh*
baby-bottle	рожок	*ruzhork*
babysitter	няня	*nyarnya*
back (at the)	сзади	*s-zardi*
back	спина	*speenah*
backpack	станковый рюкзак	*stunkorvy ryookzark*
bad	плохой	*plukhoy*
bag	сумка	*soomka*
baker	булочная	*booluchnaya*
balcony	балкон	*bulkorn*
ball	мяч	*myach*
ballet	балет	*bullyet*
ballpoint pen	шариковая ручка	*sharikuvvaya roochka*
banana	банан	*bunnarn*
bandage	бинт	*beent*
bank (river)	берег	*byayrek*
bank pass	банковский	*barnkuffski*
	паспорт	*parsspurt*
bar (café)	бар	*barr*
bar (drinks' cabinet)	бар	*barr*
barbecue	барбекю	*barbikyoo*
basketball (to play)	играть в баскетбол	*eegrart v buskitborl*
bath	ванна	*varn-na*
bath foam	пена для ванн	*pyenna dlya varn*
bath towel	банное полотенце	*barn-noye pullutyentseh*
bathing cap	купальная шапочка	*kooparlnaya sharpuchka*
bathing cubicle	раздевалка	*ruzdivarlka*
bathing suit	купальник	*kooparlnik*
bathroom	ванная	*varn-naya*
battery	батарейка	*butturryayka*
battery	аккумулятор	*akoomoolyartur*
beach	пляж	*plyash*
beans (white)	бобы (белые)	*bubby (byely-yeh)*
beautiful	красивый	*krusseevy*

beautiful	прекрасный	*prikrarsny*
beauty parlour	косметический	*kussmeteecheski*
	салон	*sullorn*
bed	кровать	*kruvvart*
bedbug	клоп	*klorp*
bee	пчела	*pchillar*
beef	говядина	*guvvyardina*
beer	пиво	*peeva*
beetroot	свёкла	*svyokla*
begin	начать	*nuchart*
beginner	новичок	*nuvvichork*
behind	за	*zah*
below	внизу	*vneezoo*
belt	пояс	*por-yus*
belt	ремень	*rimyen*
bench	скамейка	*skummyayka*
berth	спальное место	*sparlnoye myesta*
better	лучше	*loochsha*
bicycle	велосипед	*villussipyet*
bicycle pump	велосипедный	*villussipyedny*
	насос	*nussorss*
bicycle repairs	ремонт	*rimornt*
	велосипедов	*villussipyeduff*
bikini	бикини	*beekeeni*
bill	счёт	*shchot*
billiards (to play)	играть в бильярд	*eegrart vbilyart*
birthday	день рождения	*dyen ruzhdyayniya*
birthday party	именины	*eemineeny*
biscuit	бисквит	*beeskveet*
bite	укусить	*ookoosseet*
bitter	горький	*gorki*
black	чёрный	*chorny*
bland	безвкусный	*byesfkoosny*
blanket	одеяло	*uddiyarla*
bleach (vb)	обесцветить	*ubbyestvyeteet*
blister	волдырь	*vuldyr*
block of flats	многоэтажный дом	*mnorga-etarzny dorm*

blonde	белокурый	*byelokoory*
blood	кровь	*krorv*
blood pressure	давление крови	*duvvlyayniyeh krorvi*
blouse	блуза	*blooza*
blow dry	сушить феном	*soosheet fyenum*
blue	синий	*seeni*
blunt	тупой	*toopoy*
boat	лодка	*lortka*
body	тело	*tyela*
body milk	молочко	*mulluchkor*
boiled	варёный	*vurryony*
boiled ham	окорок	*orkurruk*
bonnet	капот	*kupport*
book (vb)	зарезервировать	*zarezairvee-ruvvart*
book	Книга	*kneega*
book, order (vb)	заказать	*zukkuzzart*
booked	заказанный	*zukkarzunny*
booking office	билетная касса	*beelyetnaya karssa*
bookshop	книжный магазин	*kneezhny mugguzzeen*
border	граница	*grunneetsa*
bored (to be)	скучать	*skoochart*
boring	скучный	*skooshny*
born	рождённый	*ruzhdyonny*
boss	начальник	*nucharlnik*
botanical gardens	ботанический сад	*botaneecheski sart*
both	оба	*orba*
bottle	бутылка	*bootylka*
box (in theatre)	ложа	*lorzha*
box	коробка	*kurrorpka*
boy	мальчик	*marlchik*
bra	лифчик	*leefchik*
bracelet	браслет	*brusslyet*
braised	тушёный	*tooshony*
brake	тормоз	*tormuss*
brake fluid	тормозная жидкость	*turmuznahya zhitkust*
bread	хлеб	*khlyep*

break (leg)	сломать (ногу)	*slummart (norgoo)*
breakdown	неисправность	*nyeh-eesprarvnust*
breakfast	завтрак	*zarftruk*
breast	грудь	*groot*
bridge	мост	*morst*
briefs	трусы	*troossy*
bring	принести	*preenistee*
broadcast	передача	*piridarcha*
brochure	брошюра	*brushoora*
broken	сломанный	*slormunny*
broth	бульон	*boolyorn*
brother	брат	*brart*
brown	коричневый	*kurreechnyevy*
bruise (vb)	ушибить	*ooshibeet*
brush	щётка	*shchotka*
Brussels sprouts	брюссельская	*bryoosyellskaya*
	капуста	*kuppoosta*
bucket	ведро	*vidror*
building	здание	*zdarniyeh*
buoy	буй	*booy*
burglary	взлом	*vzlorm*
burn (n)	ожог	*uzhork*
burn	гореть	*gurryayt*
burnt	пригорелый	*preegurryely*
bus	автобус	*ufftorboos*
bus station	автовокзал	*arftavukkzarl*
bus stop	остановка автобуса	*ustunnorfka ufftorboosa*
business class	бизнес-класс	*beeznyess-klarss*
business trip	деловая поездка	*dyelluvvahya puyestka*
busy	занятый	*zarnyaty*
butane camping gas	бутан	*bootarn*
butcher	мясной магазин	*myassnoy mugguzzeen*
butter	масло	*marsla*
buttered roll	булочка (с маслом)	*booluchka (smarsslum)*
button	пуговица	*pooguveetsa*
button (on appliance)	кнопка	*knorpka*
buy	купить	*koopeet*

C

cabbage	капуста	*kapoosta*
cabin	каюта	*kayoota*
café	кафе	*kuff-eh*
cake	пирожное	*peerorzhnoyeh*
cake	торт	*tort*
cake shop	кондитер	*kundeetyer*
cake biscuit	печенье	*pichaynyeh*
called (to be)	меня/его/её зовут	*minya yivvor/yiyor zuvvoot*
camera	фотоаппарат	*futta-uppurrart*
camp (vb)	жить в палатке	*zhit fpullartkyeh*
camp shop	магазин	*mugguzzeen*
camp site	кемпинг	*kyempink*
camper	кемпер	*kyempyer*
campfire	костёр	*kustyor*
camping guide	путеводитель	*pootyevuddeetyel*
	по кемпингу	*puh kyempingoo*
camping permit	разрешение на	*ruzzrishayniyeh nah*
	кемпинг	*kyempink*
canal boat	прогулочный катер	*pruggooluchny kartyer*
cancel	аннулировать	*unnooleeruvvart*
candle	свеча	*svyichar*
canoe (vb)	грести на байдарке	*gristee nah bighdarkyeh*
canoe	байдарка	*bighdarka*
canvas	холст	*khorlst*
car	машина	*mushina*
car	вагон	*vuggorn*
car breakdown	поломка мотора	*pullormka muttora*
car deck	автомобильная	*ufftummubeelnaya*
	палуба	*parlooba*
car documents	паспорт	*parsspurt*
	автомобиля	*ufftummubeelya*
car trouble	неудача	*nyeoodarcha*
carafe	графин	*gruffeen*
caravan	автоприцеп/	*arftapreetsep/*
	караван	*kurruhvarn*

cardigan	жилет	*zhilyet*
careful	осторожный	*usturrorzhny*
carton	блок	*blork*
cartridge	кассета	*kussyeta*
cascade	водопад	*vuddupart*
cash desk	касса	*karssa*
casino	казино	*kazeenor*
cassette	кассета	*kussyeta*
castle	замок	*zarmuk*
cat	кошка	*korshka*
catalogue	каталог	*kuttullork*
cathedral	собор	*subbor*
cauliflower	цветная капуста	*tsvitnahya kupoosta*
cave	пещера	*pishchaira*
CD	компакт-диск	*kumparkt-deesk*
celebrate	пировать	*peeruvvart*
cellotape	клейкая лента	*klyaykaya lyenta*
cemetery	кладбище	*klardbeeshcheh*
centimetre	сантиметр	*sunteemyetr*
central heating	центральное	*tsentrarlnoyeh*
	отопление	*uttuplyayniyeh*
centre	в середине	*fsirideenyeh*
centre	центр	*tsentr*
chair	стул	*stool*
chambermaid	горничная	*gornichnaya*
champagne	шампанское	*shumparnskoyeh*
change (trains etc)	пересесть	*pirisyest*
change (vb)	изменить	*eezmineet*
change (money)	обменять	*ubbminyart*
change the baby's nappy	перепеленать	*piripillinart*
change the oil	сменить масло	*smineet marssla*
chapel	часовня	*chussorvnya*
charter flight	чартерный рейс	*charterny rayss*
chat up	кадрить	*kuddreet*
check	проверить	*pruvvayreet*
check in	прокомпостировать	*prukkumpus*
	билет	*teeruvvat beelyet*

cheers	за здоровье	*zah zdurrorvyeh*
cheese	сыр	*syr*
chemist	аптека	*uptyeka*
cheque	чек	*chyek*
cherries	вишни	*veeshni*
chess	играть в шахматы	*eegrart vsharkhmutty*
chewing gum	жвачка	*zhvarchka*
chicken	курица	*kooritsa*
chicory	цикорий	*tsikori*
child	ребёнок	*ribyonuk*
child's car seat	детское сидение	*dyetskoye seedyayniyeh*
child's seat	детское седло	*dyetskoyeh siddlor*
chilled	прохладный	*prukhlardny*
chin	подбородок	*puddburrorduk*
chips	жареная картошка	*zharyenaya kartorshka*
chocolate	шоколад	*shokullart*
choose	выбрать	*vybrat*
chop	отбивная котлета	*utbivnaya kuttlyetta*
christian name	имя	*eemya*
church	церковь	*tsairkuf*
church service	(церковная)	*(tsirkorvnaya)*
	служба	*sloozhba*
cigar	сигара	*seegara*
cigarette	сигарета	*seegurryeta*
cigarette paper	промокашка	*prummukkarshka*
ciné camera	киноаппарат	*keena-uppurrart*
circle	круг	*krook*
circus	цирк	*tsirk*
city map	схема	*skhyema*
classical concert	классический	*klasseechiskee*
	концерт	*kuntsairt*
clean (vb)	почистить	*pucheesteet*
clean	чистый	*cheesty*
clear	ясный	*yarsny*
clearance	уборка	*ooborka*
closed	закрытый	*zukkryty*
closed off	закрыт	*zukkryt*

clothes	одежда	*uddyezhda*
clothes hanger	плечики	*plyaychiki*
clothes peg	прищепка	preeshchepka
clothing	одежда	*uddyezhda*
coat	пальто	*parltor*
cockroach	таракан	*turrukkarn*
cocoa	какао	*kukkah-oh*
cod	треска	*triskar*
coffee	кофе	*korfyeh*
coffee filter	фильтр (для кофе)	*feeltr (dlya korfyeh)*
cognac	коньяк	*kunnyak*
cold (n)	насморк	*narsmurk*
cold	холодный	*khullordny*
cold cuts	мясные изделия	*myissny-yeh eezdyayliya*
collarbone	ключица	*klyoocheetsa*
colleague	коллега	*kullyega*
collision	столкновение	*stulknuvvyayniyeh*
cologne	одеколон	*uddikullorn*
colour	цвет	*tsvyet*
colour pencils	цветные карандаши	*tsvitny-yeh kurrun dushee*
colour TV	цветной телевизор	*tsvitnoy tyeleveezor*
colouring book	альбом для раскрашивания	*arlborm dlya raskrarshivarniya*
comb	расчёска	*raschoska*
come	прийти/приехать	*preetee/preeyekhat*
come back	вернуться	*virnootsa*
complaint	жалоба	*zharlubba*
complaints book	книга жалоб	*kneega zharlupp*
completely	совсем	*suffsyem*
compliment	комплимент	*kumplimyent*
compulsory	обязательный	*ubbyuzzartyelny*
concert	концерт	*kuntsairt*
concert hall	концертный зал	*kuntsairtny zarl*
concussion	сотрясение мозга	*suttryasyayniye morzga*
condensed milk	концентрированное молоко	*kuntsentreeruvun noyeh mullukkor*

condom	презерватив	*prezairvutteeff*
congratulate	поздравлять	*puzdruvvlyart*
connection	связь	*svyarss*
constipation	запор	*zuppor*
consulate	консульство	*kornsoolstva*
consultation	консультация	*kunnsooltartsiya*
contact lens	контактная линза	*kunntarktnaya leenza*
contact lens solution	жидкость для	*zhitkust dlya*
	контактных линз	*kunntarktnykh leens*
contagious	заразный	*zurrarzny*
contraceptive	противозачаточное	*prutteevozuchar*
	средство	*tuchnoyeh sryetstva*
contraceptive pill	противозачаточные	*prutteevozuchar*
	таблетки	*tuchny-yeh tubblyetki*
cook (vb)	готовить	*guttorveet*
cook	повар	*porvur*
copper	медь	*myed*
copy	копия	*korpiya*
corkscrew	штопор	*shtorpur*
corner	угол	*oogul*
correct	правильный	*prarveelny*
correspond	переписываться	*piripeessyvvutsa*
corridor	коридор	*kurreedor*
cot	детская кроватка	*dyetskaya kruvvartka*
cotton	хлопок	*khlorpuk*
cotton wool	вата	*varta*
cough	кашель	*karshel*
cough mixture	микстура от кашля	*mikstoora ut karshlya*
counter	окно	*uknor*
country	страна	*strunnah*
country (village)	деревня	*diryevnya*
country code	код страны	*kort strunny*
courgette	кабачок	*kubbuchork*
course of treatment	лечение	*lichayniyeh*
cousin (female)	двоюродная сестра	*dvuhyoorudnaya syistrar*
cousin (male)	двоюродный брат	*dvuyoorudny brart*
crab	краб	*krarp*

crayfish	рак	*rark*
cream	сливки	*sleefki*
credit card	кредитная	*kredeetnaya*
	карточка	*kartuchka*
crisps	чипсы	*cheepsy*
cross-country run	лыжная трасса	*lyzhnaya trarssa*
cross-country skiing	кататься на лыжах	*kuttartsa nah lyzhakh*
cross-country skis	лыжи	*lyzhi*
cross the road	перейти	*pireetee*
crossing	переправа	*piriprarva*
crossing	перекрёсток	*pirikryostuk*
cry	плакать	*plarkat*
cubic metre	кубический метр	*koobeecheski myetr*
cucumber	огурец	*uggooryets*
cuddly toy	плюшевая игрушка	*plyooshevaya eegrooshka*
cufflinks	запонки	*zarpunki*
culottes	юбка-брюки	*yoopka-bryooki*
cup	чашка	*charshka*
curly	вьющийся	*v-yooshchiysya*
current	течение	*tichayniyeh*
cushion	подушечка	*puddooshuchka*
custard	крем	*kryem*
customary	обычно	*ubbychna*
customs	таможня	*tummorzhnya*
customs inspection	таможенный	*tummorzhinny*
	досмотр	*dusmortr*
cut (vb)	резать	*ryezart*
cutlery	прибор	*preebor*

dairy produce	молочные продукты	*mullorchny-yeh pruddookty*
damaged	повреждённый	*puvvrizhdyonny*
dance	танцевать	*tuntsivart*
danger	опасность	*upparsnust*
dangerous	опасный	*upparsny*
dark	тёмный	*tyomny*
date (rendezvous)	встреча	*fstraycha*
daughter	дочь	*dorch*
day (hrs)	сутки	*sootki*
day	день	*dyen*
day after tomorrow	послезавтра	*porslizarftra*
day before yesterday	позавчера	*puzzufchirar*
dead	мёртвый	*myortvy*
dear (sweet)	милый	*meely*
decaffeinated	без кофеина	*byes kuffayeena*
December	декабрь	*dyekarbr*
deck chair	шезлонг	*shezlornk*
declare (customs)	предъявить на таможне	*prid-yaveet nah tummorzhneh*
deep	глубокий	*glooborki*
deep sea diving	подводное плавание	*puddvordnoyeh plarvunniyeh*
deepfrozen	замороженный	*zummurrorzhinny*
degrees	градусы	*grardoosy*
delay	задержка	*zuddyershka*
delicious	вкусный	*fkoosny*
delicious	великолепный	*vyelikullyepny*
dentist	зубной врач	*zoobnoy vrarch*
dentures	зубной протез	*zoobnoy pruttess*
deodorant	дезодорант	*dezuddurrarnt*
department	отдел	*utdyel*
department store	универмаг	*ooneevairmark*
departure	отъезд	*utt-yest*
departure time	время отправления	*vraymya utpruvvlyayniya*

depilatory cream	средство для удаления волос	sryetstva dlya oodalyayniya vullorss
deposit	залог	zullork
dessert	десерт	dyissairt
destination	конец маршрута	kunnyets marshroota
destination	назначение	naznuchayniyeh
develop	проявить	pruhyuvveet
diabetic	диабетик	deeabbaytik
dial	набрать	nubbrart
diamond	алмаз	ullmarss
diarrhoea	понос	punnorss
diarrhoea treatment	лекарство от поноса	likarstva ut punnorssa
dictionary	словарь	sluvvar
diesel	дизель	deezil
diesel oil	дизельное масло	deezilnoyeh marslo
diet	диета	diyeta
difficulty	сложность	slorzhnust
dining room	столовая	stullorvaya
dining/buffet car	вагон-ресторан	vuggorn-risturrarn
dinner (to have)	ужинать	oozhinnart
dinner	ужин	oozhin
dinner jacket	смокинг	smorkink
direct	прямой	pryummoy
direction	направление	nuppruvlyayniyeh
dirty	грязный	gryazny
disabled	инвалид	eenvulleet
disappearance	исчезновение	eescheznuvv yayniyeh
disco	дискотека	deeskutyeka
discount	скидка	skeetka
dish	блюдо	blyooda
dish of the day	дежурное блюдо	dyezhoornoyeh blyooda
disinfectant	дезинфицирующее средство	dyezeenfitseerooy ooshcheh-yeh sryetstva
distance	расстояние	rus-stuyarniyeh
distilled water	дистиллированная вода	distileerorvunnaya vuddar

disturb	помешать	*pummishart*
dive	нырять	*nyryart*
diving	водолазный спорт	*vuddullarzny sport*
diving board	трамплин	*trumpleen*
diving gear	водолазные	*vuddullarzny-yeh*
	принадлежности	*preenudlyayzhnusti*
divorced	разведён	*ruzvidyon*
	(разведена)	*(ruzvidyinar)*
DIY-shop	магазин	*mugguzzeen*
	«сделай сам»	*"zdyelay sarm"*
dizzy	у меня кружится	*oo minya kroozhit*
	голова	*sa gulluvvar*
do	делать	*dyellut*
doctor	врач	*vrarch*
dog	собака	*subbarka*
doll	кукла	*kookla*
domestically	внутри страны	*vnootree strunny*
(inside country)		
done (cooked)	варёный	*vurryony*
door	дверь	*dvyair*
double	двухместный	*dvookhmyestny*
draught (there is a)	сквозить	*skvuzzeet*
draughts (to play)	играть , шашки	*eegrart fsharshki*
dream	мечтать	*michtart*
dress	платье	*plartyeh*
dressing gown	халат	*khullart*
drink (n)	напиток	*nuppeetuk*
drink	пить	*peet*
drinking water	питьевая вода	*peetyivaya vuddah*
drive (vb)	ехать	*yekhat*
driver	шофёр	*shuffyor*
driving licence	водительские	*vuddeetyelskiyeh*
	права	*pruvvar*
drought	засуха	*zarssookhah*
drugs	наркотики	*narkortiki*
dry	сушить	*soosheet*
dry	сухой	*sookhoy*

dry clean	почистить	*pucheesteet*
dry cleaner's	(хим)чистка	*(khim)cheestka*
dry shampoo	сухой шампунь	*sookhoy shumpoon*
dummy	пустышка	*poostyshka*
during	в течение	*ftichayniyeh*
during the day	днём	*dnyom*

E

ear	ухо	*ookha*
ear nose and throat (ENT) specialist	ушной врач	*ooshnoy vrarch*
ear-ache	боль в ухе	*borl vookhyeh*
ear-drops	ушные капли	*ooshny-yeh karpli*
early	рано	*rarna*
earrings	серьги	*syairgee*
earth	земля	*zimlyah*
earthenware	посуда	*pussooda*
east	восток	*vustork*
easy	лёгкий	*lyokhki*
eat	есть	*yest*
eczema	экзема	*ekzemma*
eel	угорь	*oogur*
egg	яйцо	*yightsor*
elastic band	резинка	*rizeenka*
electric	электрический	*eliktreecheski*
electricity	ток	*tork*
embassy	посольство	*pussorlstva*
emergency brake	запасной тормоз	*zuppussnoy tormuss*
emergency exit	запасной выход	*zuppussnoy vykhut*
emergency phone	аварийный телефон	*avurreeny tyeliforn*
emergency triangle	знак аварийной остановки	*znark uvvureenoy usttunnorfki*
empty	пустой	*poostoy*
engaged (of telephone)	занят	*zarnyat*

engaged	занятый	*zarnyaty*
England	Англия	***Arn**gliya*
English (adj)	английский	*un**glee**ski*
Englishman	англичанин	*unglich**arn**in*
Englishwoman	англичанка	*unglich**arn**ka*
enjoy	наслаждаться	*nussluzhd**arts**a*
envelope	конверт	*kunn**vyairt***
evening (in the)	вечером	*vaychirum*
evening	вечер	*vaychir*
evening wear	вечерняя одежда	*vich**air**nyaya udd**ye**zhda*
event	событие	*sub**by**tiyeh*
everything	всё	*fsyo*
everywhere	везде	*vizd**yeh***
examine	осмотреть	*ussmutt**rayt***
excavation	раскопки	*ras**kor**pki*
excellent	отличный	*utt**leech**ny*
exchange	обменять	*ubmin**yart***
exchange office	пункт обмена	*poonkt ubbm**ye**na*
	валюты	*vull**yoo**ty*
exchange rate	курс	*koorss*
excursion	экскурсия	*eks**koo**rsiya*
exhibition	выставка	*vystuffka*
exit	выход	*vykhudd*
expenses	расходы	*russkh**or**dy*
expensive	дорогой	*durrugg**oy***
explain	объяснить	*ubb-yuss**neet***
express train	скорый поезд	*skory por-yist*
external	внешний	*vn**ye**shni*
eye	глаз	*glarss*
eyedrops	глазные капли	*gluzzny-yeh karpli*
eyeshadow	тени (для глаз)	***tyay**ni (dlya glarss)*
eye specialist	глазной врач	*gluzz**noy** vrarch*
eyeliner	карандаш для	*kurrund**arsh** dlya*
	обводки глаз	*ub**vor**tki glarss*

F

face	лицо	*leetsor*
factory	завод	*zuvvort*
fair	балаганы	*bulluggarny*
faith	вера	*vyaira*
fall	упасть	*ooparst*
family	семья	*sim-yar*
famous	знаменитый	*znammineety*
far away	далёкий	*dullyoki*
farm	ферма	*fyairma*
farmer	крестьянин	*krist-yarnin*
farmer's wife	крестьянка	*krist-yanka*
fashion	мода	*morda*
fast	быстрый	*bystry*
father	отец	*uttyets*
fault	вина	*veenar*
fax (vb)	отослать факс	*uttusslart farks*
February	февраль	*fivvrarl*
feel	чувствовать	*choostvuvvart*
feel like	хотеть	*khuttyayt*
ferry	паром	*purrorm*
fill (tooth)	пломбировать	*plumbeerruvvart*
fill out	заполнить	*zupporlneet*
filling	пломба	*plormba*
film	фильм	*feelm*
filter	фильтр	*feeltr*
find	найти	*nigh-tee*
fine	штраф	*shtrarf*
finger	палец	*parlyets*
fire	огонь	*uggorn*
fire	пожар	*puzhar*
fire brigade	пожарная команда	*puzharnaya kummarnda*
fire escape	пожарная лестница	*puzharnaya lyessnitsa*
fire extinguisher	огнетушитель	*ugnyetoosheetyel*

first	первый	*pyairvy*
first aid	скорая помощь	*skoraya pormushch*
first class	первый класс	*pyairvy klarss*
fish (vb)	ловить рыбу	*luvveet ryboo*
fish	рыба	*ryba*
fishing rod	удочка	*ooduchka*
fitness centre	спортивно-оздоровительный центр	*spurteevna-uzdur raveetyelny tsentr*
fitness training	спортивно-оздоровительная тренировка	*spurteevna-uzdur raveetyelnaya tre neerorfka*
fitting room	примерочная	*preemyairuchnaya*
fix (stick together)	заклеить	*zukklyayeet*
flag	флаг	*flark*
flash	вспышка	*fspyshka*
flash bulb	лампочка для вспышки	*larmpuchka dlya fspyshki*
flea market	барахолка	*burrukhorlka*
flight	полёт	*pullyot*
flight number	рейс	*rayss*
flood	наводнение	*nuvvudnyayniyeh*
floor	пол	*porl*
floor	этаж	*etarzh*
flour	мука	*mookar*
'flu	грипп	*greep*
flyover	путепровод	*pootyehpruvvort*
fly (insect)	муха	*mookha*
fly (vb)	лететь	*lityayt*
fog	туман	*toomarn*
foggy (to be)	стоит туман	*stuh-eet toomarn*
folkloristic	фольклорный	*folklorny*
follow	последовать	*pusslyayduvvart*
food	пища	*peeshcha*
food	продукты	*pruddookty*
food poisoning	пищевое отравление	*peeshchivvor-yeh uttruvvlyayniyeh*

foot	нога	*nuggar*
for hire	сдаётся	*zdayotsa*
forbidden	запрещён	*zupprishchon*
forehead	лоб	*lorp*
foreign	иностранный	*eenustrarny*
forget	забыть	*zubbyt*
fork	вилка	*veelka*
form	бланк	*blarnk*
fort	крепость	*kryepust*
forward (vb)	переслать	*pirislart*
fountain	фонтан	*funtarn*
four-star	бензин высшего качества	*binzeen vys-shuv va karchistva*
frame	оправа	*upprarva*
franc	франк	*frarnk*
free	свободный	*svubbordny*
free (gratis)	бесплатный	*byesplartny*
free time	свободное время	*svubbordnoyeh vraymya*
freeze	морозить	*murrorzeet*
French	французский	*frunntsooski*
French bread	батон	*buttorn*
fresh	свежий	*svyayzhi*
Friday	пятница	*pyartnitsa*
fried	жареный	*zharinny*
fried egg	(яичница-)глазунья	*(ya-eeshnitsa-)gluzzoonya*
fried eggs	яичница	*ya-eeshnitsa*
friend	друг	*drook*
friendly	сердечный	*sairdyaychny*
friendly	любезный	*lyoobyezny*
frightened	боязливый	*buyazleevy*
fringe	чёлка	*cholka*
fruit	фрукты	*frookty*
fruit juice	фруктовый сок	*frooktorvy sork*
frying pan	сковорода	*skuvvurruddar*
full	полный	*porlny*
fun	удовольствие	*ooduvvorlstveeyeh*
fun	забавный	*zubbarvny*

gallery	галерея	*galliraya*
game	игра	*eegrar*
garage	гараж	*gurrarsh*
garbage bag	мусорный мешок	*moosorny mishork*
garden	сад	*sart*
gastroenteritis	расстройство	*rus-stroystva zhilootka*
	желудка и кишок	*ee keeshork*
gate in fence	калитка	*kulleetka*
gauze	марля	*marlya*
gel	гель	*gell*
German	немецкий	*nimyetskiy*
get hold of	достать	*dustart*
get married (m)	жениться	*zhinneetsa*
get married (f)	выйти замуж	*vytee zarmoozh*
get off	выйти	*vytee*
gift	подарок	*puddaruk*
gilt	позолоченный	*puzzullorchunny*
ginger	имбирь	*imbeer*
girl	девочка	*dyevuchka*
girlfriend	подруга	*pudrooga*
giro cheque	жироприказ	*zheeropreekarss*
giro pass	жиропас	*zheeroparss*
glacier	ледник	*lyidneek*
glass (tumbler)	стакан	*stukkarn*
glass (vodka)	рюмка	*ryoomka*
glass (wine-)	бокал	*bukkarl*
glasses (sun-)	очки	*uchkee*
glide	лететь на планёре	*lityayt nah plunnyoryeh*
glove	перчатка	*pirchartka*
glue	клей	*klyay*
gnat	комар	*kummar*
go	идти/ехать	*eed-tee/yekhat*
go back	вернуться	*virnootsa*
go out	прогуляться	*pruggoolyartsa*
goat's cheese	козий сыр	*korzee syr*

gold	золото	*zorlutta*
golf course	площадка для	*plushchartka dlya*
	игры в гольф	*eegry vgorlf*
golf stockings	гольфы	*gorlfy*
good afternoon	добрый день	*dorbry dyen*
good evening	добрый вечер	*dorbry vyaychir*
good morning	доброе утро	*dorbroye ootra*
good night	спокойной ночи	*spukkoyny norchi*
goodbye (n)	прощание	*prushcharniye*
goodbye	до свидания	*duh sveedarniya*
gram	грамм	*grarm*
grandchild	,нук (внучка)	*vnook (vnoochka)*
grandfather	дедушка	*dyedooshka*
grandmother	бабушка	*barbooshka*
grape juice	виноградный сок	*veenugrardny sork*
grapefruit	грейпфрут	*graypfroot*
grapes	виноград	*veenugrart*
grave	могила	*mugeela*
greasy	жирный	*zheerny*
green	зелёный	*zillyony*
greet	здороваться	*zdurrorvatsa*
grey	серый	*syairy*
grey (of hair)	седой	*sidoy*
grill	жарить на вертеле	*zharit nah vyairtyelyeh*
grilled	жареный на	*zhariny nah*
	вертеле	*vyairtyelyeh*
grocer's	бакалейный	*bukkullyayny*
	магазин	*mugguzzeen*
group	группа	*groopa*
guest house	пансион	*punnseeorn*
guide (book)	путеводитель	*pootyevuddeetyel*
guide (person)	гид	*geet*
guided tour	экскурсия	*ekskoorsiya*
gynaecologist	гинеколог	*geenyekorlukk*

H

hair	волосы	*vorlussy*
hair-do	причёска	*preechoska*
hairbrush	щётка	*shchotka*
hairdresser	парикмахерская (женская мужская)	*parikmarkherskaya*
hairpins	шпильки	*shpeelki*
hairspray	лак для волос	*lark dlya vullorss*
half (advb)	наполовину	*napulluvveenoo*
half	половина	*pulluveena*
half a kilo	полкило	*pullkeelor*
half full	полупустой	*pulloopoostoy*
hammer	молоток	*mulluttork*
hand	рука	*rookar*
handbrake	ручной тормоз	*roochnoy tormuss*
handbag	сумка	*soomka*
handkerchief	носовой платок	*nussuvvoy pluttork*
handmade	сделанный вручную	*zdyelunny vroochnooyu*
happy	рад (рада)	*raht (rarda)*
harbour	порт	*port*
hard	твёрдый	*tvyordy*
hat	шляпа	*shlyarpa*
hayfever	сенная лихорадка	*syinnahya likhurratka*
hazelnut	лесной орех	*lyissnoy urryekh*
head	голова	*gulluvvar*
headache	головная боль	*gulluvnahya borl*
health	здоровье	*zdurrorvyeh*
health food shop	магазин натуральных продуктов	*mugguzzeen nut toorarlnykh*
hear	слышать	*slyshart*
hearing aid	слуховой аппарат	*slookhuvvoy uppurrart*
heart	сердце	*sairtseh*
heart patient	у него больное сердце	*oo nyivvor bullnor-yeh sairtseh*

heater	отопление	*uttuplyayniyeh*
heavy	тяжёлый	*tyuzholly*
heel	пятка	*pyartka*
heel	каблук	*kablook*
hello	здравствуйте	*zdrarstvooytyeh*
hello (colloquial)	привет	*preevyet*
helmet	шлем	*shlyem*
help (vb)	помочь	*pummorch*
help!	помощь	*pormushch*
helping	порция	*portseeya*
herbal tea	чай из трав	*chigh ees trahf*
here	здесь	*zdyess*
herring	селёдка	*silyotka*
high	высокий	*vyssorki*
high tide	прилив	*preeleef*
highchair	детский стульчик	*dyetski stoolchik*
hiking	пешеходный	*pishikhordny*
	туризм	*tooreezm*
hiking trip	поход	*pukhort*
hip	бедро	*byidror*
hire	снять	*snyat*
hitchhike	путешествовать	*pootyeshestvuvvart*
	автостопом	*arftostorpum*
hobby	хобби	*khorbi*
hold-up	налёт	*nullyot*
holiday	отпуск	*ortpoosk*
holiday house	дача	*darcha*
home (at)	дома	*dorma*
homesickness	тоска по родине	*tusskar puh rordeenyeh*
honest	честный	*chaystny*
honey	мёд	*myot*
honeydew melon	дыня	*dynya*
horizontal	горизонтальный	*gurreezuntarlny*
horrible	отвратительный	*utvrateetyulny*
horse	лошадь	*lorshut*
hospital	больница	*bullneetsa*
hospitality	гостеприимство	*gostipree-eemstva*

hot-water bottle	грелка	*gryelka*
hotel	гостиница	*gusteenitsa*
hour	час	*charss*
house	дом	*dorm*
household items	хозяйственные товары	*khuzyigh-stvunny-yeh tuvvary*
houses of parliament	здание парламента	*zdarniyeh parlarmyenta*
housewife	домохозяйка	*dormakhuzzyighka*
how far?	как далеко?	*kukk dullikor?*
how long?	как долго?	*kukk dorlga?*
how much?	сколько?	*skorlka?*
how?	как?	*kark?*
hundred grams	сто грамм	*stor grarm*
hunger	голод	*gorlut*
hurricane	ураган	*ooruggarn*
hurry (n)	поспешность	*puspyeshnust*
husband	муж	*moozh*
hut	избушка	*eezbooshka*
hyperventilation	гипервентиляция	*geeperventeelyatsiya*

I

ice cubes	кубики льда	*koobeeki l-dah*
ice skates	коньки	*kunkee*
ice-cream	мороженое	*murrorzhinoyeh*
idea	идея	*eedyaya*
identification	удостоверение личности	*oodustuvviryayniyeh leechnusti*
identify	установить личность	*oostunnuvveet leechnust*
ignition key	ключ зажигания	*klyooch zuzhigarniya*
ill	больной	*bullnoy*
illness	болезнь	*bullyezn*
imagine	представить себе	*pridstarveet sibbyeh*
immediately	непосредственный	*nyehpussraydstvinny*
import duty	пошлина	*porshlina*
impossible	невозможный	*nyehvuzzmorzhny*

in	в	v
in front of	перед	p**yay**rut
included	включая	fkly**oo**ch**ah**ya
indicate	показать	pukk**uzz**art
indicator	указатель	ook**uzz**artyel
	поворота	puvv**urr**orta
inexpensive	дешёвый	dish**or**vy
infection	заражение	zurruzh**ay**niyeh
inflammation	воспаление	vusspull**yay**niyeh
information	информация	eenform**art**siyah
information office	справочное бюро	spr**ar**vuchnoyeh by**oo**ror
injection	укол	ook**orl**
injured	раненый	r**arn**yunny
inner tube	камера шины	**kar**myera sh**iny**
innocent	невинный	nyehv**ee**ny
insect	насекомое	nussik**or**moye
insect bite	укус насекомого	ook**oos** nussik**or**muvva
insect repellant	масло против	**mar**slo pr**or**teef
	комаров	kummar**orff**
inside	внутри	vn**oo**tree
insole	стелька	st**ye**lka
instructions	правила	pr**ar**veela
	пользования	p**or**lzuvvunniya
insurance	страхование	strukhuvv**ar**niyeh
intermission	перерыв	pirir**yff**
international	международный	myezhdoonurr**or**dny
interpreter	переводчик	piriv**or**tchik
introduce oneself	представиться	prid**star**veetsa
invite	пригласить	preegluss**eet**
iodine	йод	yot
Ireland	Ирландия	Eerl**arn**deeya
Irish (adj)	ирландский	eerl**arn**ski
Irishman	ирландец	eerl**arn**dyets
Irishwoman	ирландка	eerl**arn**tka
iron	железо	zhil**yay**za
iron	гладить	gl**ar**deet
iron (metal)	утюг	oot**yook**

ironing board	гладильная доска	*glud**dee**lnaya dus**kar***
island	остров	***or**struff*
Italian	итальянский	*eetull**yar**nski*
itch	зуд	*zoot*

J

jack	домкрат	*dumkr**art***
jacket	пиджак	*pidzh**ark***
January	январь	*yun**var***
jaw	челюсть	*ch**ay**lyoost*
jeans	джинсы	*dzh**ee**nssy*
jellyfish	медуза	*mid**oo**za*
jeweller	ювелир	*yoovel**eer***
jewellery	драгоценности	*draggots**e**nusti*
jog	бегать	*b**ye**gart*
joke	шутка	*sh**oo**tka*
juice	сок	*sork*
July	июль	*eey**oo**l*
jumble sale	барахолка	*burrakh**or**lka*
jump leads	электропровод	*elektropr**or**vut*
	(для присоединения	*(dlya preesuhyid*
	присоединения к	*in**yay**niya kuk**koo***
	аккумулятору	*mool**yah**-turroo*
	другой машины)	*droog**oy** mushiny)*
jumper	свитер	*s**vee**ter*
June	июнь	*eey**oo**n*

key	ключ(ик)	*klyooch(ik)*
kilo	кило	*keelor*
kilometre	километр	*keelommyetr*
king	король	*kurrorl*
kiss (vb)	целовать	*tsilluvvart*
kiss	поцелуй	*putsilooy*
kitchen	кухня	*kookhnya*
knee	колено	*kullyayno*
knickers	трусики	*troosikki*
knife	нож	*norsh*
knit	вязать	*vyazart*
know	знать	*znart*

L

lace	кружево	*kroozhivva*
ladies'	женский туалет	*zhenski tooullyet*
lake	озеро	*orzira*
lamp	лампа	*larmpa*
land	приземлиться	*preezimleetsa*
lane	полоса движения	*pullussar dveezhayniya*
language	язык	*yuzzyk*
lard	сало	*sarlo*
large	большой	*bullshoy*
last (previous)	прошлый	*prorshly*
last	последний	*puslaydni*
last night	прошлой ночью	*prorshloy norchyoo*
late	поздний	*porzni*
later	потом	*puttorm*
laugh (vb)	смеяться	*smeeyartsa*
launderette	прачечная	*prarchichnaya*
law	право	*prarvo*
laxative	слабительное	*slabeetyelnoyeh*
leather	кожа	*korzha*

leather goods	кожевенные товары	*kuzhevin-ny-yeh tuvvary*
leave	уехать	*ooyekhat*
leek	порей	*purray*
left (on the)	налево	*nahlyeva*
left	левый	*lyevy*
left luggage	камера хранения багажа	*karmyera khrun-nyayniya bugguzhar*
leg	нога	*nuggar*
lemon	лимон	*leemorn*
lend	дать взаймы	*dart vzigh-my*
lens	линза	*leenza*
lentils	чечевица	*chichiveetsa*
less	меньше	*myensha*
lesson	урок	*oorork*
letter	письмо	*peessmor*
lettuce	кочанный салат	*kucharn-ny sullart*
level crossing	железнодорожный переезд	*zhileyeznodur-rorzhny pireeyest*
library	библиотека	*beebliotyeka*
lie (tell lies)	лгать	*l-gart*
lie	лежать	*lizhart*
lift (hitchhike)	подвезти	*puddvistee*
lift (in building)	лифт	*leeft*
lift (ski)	кресельная канатная дорога	*kraysyelnaya kunnartnaya durrorga*
light (n)	свет	*svyet*
light (not dark)	светлый	*svyetly*
light (not heavy)	лёгкий	*lyokhki*
lighter	зажигалка	*zuzhigarlka*
lighthouse	маяк	*mayark*
lightning	молния	*morlniya*
like (I like it)	мне нравится	*mnyeh nrarvitsa*
like/love	любить	*lyoobeet*
line	линия	*leeneeya*
lipstick	губная помада	*goobnahya pummarda*
liquorice	лакрица	*lukkreetsa*

listen	слушать	*slooshat*
literature	литература	*litairatoora*
litre	литр	*leetr*
little (a)	немного	*nimnorga*
live	жить	*zhit*
live together	жить совместно	*zhit suvvmyestna*
local	местный	*myestny*
lock	замок	*zummork*
long	длинный	*dleeny*
look (vb)	смотреть	*smuttrayt*
look for	искать	*eeskart*
look round	осмотреть	*ussmuttrayt*
lorry	грузовик	*groozuvveek*
lose	потерять	*puttyiryart*
loss	потеря	*puttyairya*
lost (to be)	заблудиться	*zubbloodeetsa*
lost	потерянный	*puttyayryunny*
lost item	пропажа	*pruparzha*
lost property office	находки	*nukhortki*
lotion	лосьон	*luss-yon*
loud	громко	*grormka*
love (to be in - with)	влюблён	*vlyooblyon*
	(влюблена)	*(vlyooblinar)*
love	любовь	*lyooborf*
low	низкий	*neeski*
low tide	отлив	*uttleef*
liquid petrolium gas	сжиженный	*s-zhizhunny*
	(нефтяной) газ	*(nyeftyanoy) garss*
luck	счастье	*scharstyah*
luggage	багаж	*buggarzh*
luggage locker	багажная ячейка	*buggarzhnaya yachayka*
lumps of sugar	кусочки сахара	*koosorchki sarkhurra*
lunch	обед	*ubbyet*
lungs	лёгкие	*lyokhkeeyeh*

macaroni	макароны	*makkurorny*
machine (vending)	автомат	*ufftummart*
madam	госпожа	*gusspuzhar*
magazine	журнал	*zhoornarl*
mail	почта	*porchta*
main post office	главный почтамт	*glarvny puchtarmt*
main road	магистраль	*muggistrarl*
make an appointment	назначить свидание	*nuzznarcheet sveedarniyeh*
makeshift	временный	*vrayminny*
man	мужчина	*mooshcheena*
manager	заведующий	*zuvvyaydooyushchi*
mandarin	мандарин	*mundurreen*
manicure	маникюр	*munneekyoor*
map	карта	*karta*
map	географическая карта	*geogruffeecheskaya karta*
marble	мрамор	*mrarmur*
March	март	*mart*
margarine	маргарин	*margurreen*
marina	яхт-клуб	*yakht-kloop*
market	рынок	*rynuk*
marriage	брак	*brark*
married	женатый (замужем)	*zhinnarty (zarmoozhum)*
mass (church service)	обедня	*ubyednya*
massage	массаж	*mas-sarzh*
match (competition)	соревнование	*surrevnuvvarniyeh*
matches	спички	*speechki*
matt	матовый	*martuvvy*
May	май	*migh*
maybe	может быть	*morzhit byt*
mayonnaise	майонез	*migh-yoness*
mayor	мэр	*mair*
meal	еда	*yiddah*
mean (vb)	значить	*znarcheet*

meat	мясо	*myar*ssa
mechanical help	техпомощь	*tyekhpormushch*
media	мидия	*meediya*
medication	лекарство	*likar*stva
medicine	лекарство	*likar*stva
meet (for first time)	познакомиться	*puznukkormitsa*
membership	членство	*chlyen*stva
menstruate (vb)	у менfl	*oo minya*
	менструация	*menstrooart*siya
menstruation	менструация	*menstrooart*siya
menu	меню	*minyoo*
menu of the day	суточное меню	*sootuchnoyeh minyoo*
message	сообщение	*suh-ubbshchayniyeh*
metal	металл	*myitarl*
meter (appliance)	счётчик	*shchotchik*
metre	метр	*myetr*
migraine	мигрень	*meegryen*
mild (tobacco)	лёгкий	*lyokhki*
milk	молоко	*mullukor*
millimetre	миллиметр	*meeleemyetr*
milometer	дистанционный	*distarntsiorny*
	спидометр	*speedormyetr*
mince	рубленое мясо	*rooblyunor-yeh myarssa*
mineral water	минеральная вода	*meenirarlnaya vuddar*
minute	минута	*minoota*
mirror	зеркало	*zyairkulla*
miss (vb)	пропустить	*pruppoosteet*
missing (to be)	не хватать	*nyeh khvuttart*
mistake	ошибка	*ushipka*
mistaken (to be)	ошибиться	*ushibbeetsa*
misunderstanding	недоразумение	*nyedurrazoomyayniyeh*
modern art	современное	*suvrimmyen-noyeh*
	искусство	*eeskoostva*
moment	мгновение	*m-gnuvvayniya*
monastery	монастырь	*monnustyr*
Monday	понедельник	*punnidyelnik*

money | деньги | *dyengi* |

month	месяц	*myaysits*
moped	мопед	*muppyet*
morning	утро	*ootra*
morning (in the)	утром	*ootrum*
mosque	мечеть	*michayt*
motel	мотель	*muttayl*
mother	мать	*mart*
moto-cross	заниматься	*zannimartsa*
	мотокроссом	*muttakrorssum*
motorbike	мотоцикл	*muttatsikl*
motorboat	моторная лодка	*muttornaya lortka*
motorway	автострада	*ufftustrarda*
mountain	гора	*gurrar*
mountain hut	хижина в горах	*kheezhina vgurrahkh*
mountain-skiing	горнолыжный	*gornullyzhny*
	спорт	*sport*
mountaineering shoes	горные ботинки	*gorny-yeh butteenki*
mouse	мышь	*mysh*
mouth	рот	*rort*
much/many	много	*mnorga*
multi-storey car park	гараж (для стоянки	*gurrarzh (dlya stuyarnki*
	автомобилей)	
muscle	мышца	*myshtsa*
muscle spasms	мышечная	*myshechnaya*
	судорога	*soodurrugga*
museum	музей	*moozyay*
mushrooms	грибы	*greeby*
music	музыка	*moozyka*
musical (n)	мюзикл	*myoozikl*
mustard	горчица	*gurcheetsa*

nail (on finger)	ноготь	*nor*gut
nail	гвоздь	*gvorsst*
nail file	пилочка для	*peeluchka dlya*
	ногтей	*nukhtyay*
nail polish remover	жидкость	*zhitkust dlya*
	для снятия лака	*snyartiya*
	(с ногтей)	
nail scissors	ножницы для	*norzhneetsy dlya*
	ногтей	*nukhtyay*
naked	голый	*gorly*
nappy	пелёнка	*pilyonka*
nationality	национальность	*nutsionarlnust*
naturally	конечно	*kunnyeshna*
nature	природа	*preerorda*
naturism	нудизм	*noodeezm*
nauseous	меня тошнит	*minya tushneet*
near	близко	*bleeska*
nearby	близкий	*bleeski*
necessary	необходимый	*nyeh-ubbkhud*
		deemy
neck	шея	*shay-ya*
necklace	цепь	*tsep*
needle	игла	*eeglar*
negative	негатив	*nyegutteef*
neighbours	соседи	*sussyedi*
nephew	племянник	*plimyahnik*
never	никогда	*neekugdar*
new	новый	*norvy*
news	новость	*norvust*
news stand	киоск	*keeorsk*
newspaper	газета	*guzzyetta*
next	следующий	*slyaydooyushchi*
next to	возле	*vorzlyeh*
nice (friendly)	милый	*meely*
nice	прекрасно	*prikrarssna*

nice to eat	вкусный	*fkoosny*
niece	племянница	*plimyarnitsa*
night	ночь	*norch*
night duty	ночная смена	*nuchnaya smyena*
nightclub	ночной клуб	*nuchnoy kloop*
nightlife	ночная жизнь	*nuchnaya zhizn*
no one	никто	*neektor*
no	нет	*nyet*
no overtaking	обгон запрещён	*ubgorn zupprishchon*
noise	шум	*shoom*
nonstop	непрерывно	*nipreeryvna*
normal	обычный	*ubbychny*
normal	нормальный	*narmarlny*
north	север	*sayvir*
nose	нос	*norss*
nose drops	капли в нос	*karpli vnorss*
nosebleed	кровотечение из носа	*krorvotichayniyeh eess norsa*
notepaper	почтовая бумага	*porchtorvaya boomarga*
nothing	ничего	*nichivvor*
November	ноябрь	*nayarbr*
now	сейчас	*siycharss*
nowhere	нигде	*neegdyeh*
nudist beach	пляж нудистов	*plyarsh noodeestuff*
number	номер	*normer*
number plate	номерной знак	*nummyernoy znark*
nurse	медсестра	*myetsistrar*
nutmeg	мускатный орех	*mooskartny urryekh*
nuts	орехи	*urryekhi*

October	октябрь	*uktyarbr*
off-licence	винный магазин	*veen-ny mugguzzeen*
off (food)	испорченный	*eesporchinny*
offer	предложить	*pridluzhit*
office	контора	*kuntora*
oil	масло	*marssla*
oil level	уровень масла	*ooruvvin marssla*
ointment	мазь	*marss*
ointment for burns	мазь от ожога	*marss ut uzhorga*
okay	ладно	*lardna*
old	старый	*stary*
olive oil	оливковое масло	*ulleefkuvvoyeh marssla*
olives (green)	оливки	*ulleefki*
omelette	омлет	*umlyet*
on	на	*nah*
on board	иа борту	*nah bortoo*
on the way	в пути	*fpootee*
oncoming car	встречный автомобиль	*fstraychny ufftamubbeel*
one-way traffic	одностороннее движение	*udnusturrornyeyeh dveezhayniye*
onion	лук	*look*
open (adj)	открытый	*utkryty*
open (vb)	открыть	*utkryt*
opera	опера	*orpira*
operate	оперировать	*uppaireeruvvat*
operator (telephone)	телефонистка	*tyelifunneestka*
operetta	оперетта	*uppiretta*
opposite	напротив	*nupprorteef*
optician	оптик	*orptik*
or	или	*eeli*
orange	оранжевый	*urrarnzhivy*
orange	апельсин	*uppyelseen*
orange juice	апельсиновый сок	*uppyelseenuvvy sork*
order (in -) tidy	в порядке	*fpurryatkyeh*

order (n)	заказ	*zukkarss*
order (vb)	заказать	*zukkuzzart*
other	другие	*droogee-yeh*
other side	другая сторона	*droogahya sturrunnar*
outside	вне	*vnyeh*
over the phone	по телефону	*puh tyelifornoo*
overtake	обогнать	*ubbugnart*
oysters	устрицы	*oostritsy*

P

packed lunch	сухой паёк	*sookhoy puhyok*
page	страница	*strunneetsa*
pain	боль	*borl*
painkiller	болеутоляющее средство	*borlye-ootullyahy ooshcheyeh sryetstvo*
paint	краска	*krarska*
painting (art)	живопись	*zhivuppeess*
painting (object)	картина	*karteena*
palace	дворец	*dvurryets*
pan	кастрюля	*kustryoolya*
pancake	блин	*bleen*
pane	стекло	*styiklor*
paper	бумага	*boomarga*
paper napkin	бумажная салфетка	*boomarzhnaya sulfyetka*
paraffin oil	керосин	*kyerusseen*
parasol	зонтик	*zorntik*
parcel	посылка	*pussylka*
parcel	пакет	*pukkyet*
pardon	извините	*eezveeneetyeh*
parents	родители	*rudeetyeli*
park	парк	*park*
park	поставить машину	*pustarveet mushinoo*
parking space	стоянка (автомобилей)	*stuyarnka (uffta mubbeelyay)*
parsley	петрушка	*pitrooshka*

partner	партнёр	*partnyor*
party	вечеринка	*vyechereenka*
passable	проходимый	*prukhuddeemy*
passenger	пассажир	*pussuzheer*
passport	паспорт	*parsspurt*
passport photo	фотокарточка	*futtakartuchka*
patient	пациент	*patseeyent*
patronymic	отчество	*ortchistvo*
pavement	тротуар	*truttoo-ar*
pay	платить	*plutteet*
pay the bill	рассчитаться	*ras-schitartsa*
peach	персик	*pyairseek*
peanuts	земляные орехи	*zimlyayny-yeh urryekhi*
pear	груша	*grooshar*
peas	(зелёный) горошек	*(zillyonny) gurrorshik*
pedal	педаль	*piddarl*
pedestrian crossing	пешеходный	*pishikhordny*
	переход	*pirrikhort*
pedicure	педикюр	*pyeddikyoor*
pen	ручка	*roochka*
pencil	карандаш	*kurrundarsh*
penis	пенис	*pyeniss*
pepper	перец	*pyayrits*
performance	театральное	*tee-uttrarlnoyeh*
	представление	*pridstuvvlyayniyeh*
perfume	духи	*dookhee*
perm (verb)	сделать завивку	*zdyelat zuvveefkoo*
perm	(химическая)	*(khimeecheskaya)*
	завивка	*zuvveefka*
permit	разрешение	*ruzzrishayniyeh*
person	человек	*chilluvvyek*
personal	личный	*leechny*
petrol	бензин	*byenzeen*
petrol station	бензостанция	*byenzustarntsiya*
pets	домашние	*dummarshniyeh*
	животные	*zhivortny-yeh*
pharmacy	аптека	*uptyeka*

phone (tele-)	телефон	*tyeliforn*
phone (vb)	позвонить	*puzzvunneet*
phone box	телефонная будка	*tyeliforn-naya bootka*
phone directory	телефонная книга	*tyeliforn-naya kneega*
phone number	телефонный номер	*tyeliforn-ny normer*
photo	снимок	*sneemuk*
photocopier	ксерокс	*ksyairuks*
photocopy (n)	фотокопия	*futtakorpiya*
photocopy (vb)	делать фотокопию	*dyelat futtakorpiyu*
pick up	забрать	*zubbrart*
picnic	пикник	*peekneek*
pictures (to take)	фотографировать	*futtagruffeeruvvat*
piece of clothing	предмет одежды	*pridmyet uddyezhdy*
pier	мол	*morl*
pigeon	голубь	*gorloop*
pill (contraceptive)	противозачаточная	*prutteevuzzuchar*
	таблетка	*tuchnaya tubblyetka*
pillow	подушка	*puddooshka*
pillowcase	наволочка	*narvulluchka*
pin	булавка	*boolarfka*
pineapple	ананас	*unnunarss*
pipe	трубка	*troopka*
pipe tobacco	трубочный табак	*troobuchny tubbark*
pity	жаль	*zharl*
place of entertainment	место для	*myesta dlya*
	развлечений	*ruzzvlichayni*
place of interest	достопримеч-	*dustupprimicharty-*
	ательность	*elnust*
plan	план	*plarn*
plant	растение	*rustyayniyeh*
plasters	пластыри	*plarstyri*
plastic	пластмасса	*plustmarssa*
plastic bag	пакет	*pukkyet*
plate	тарелка	*turryelka*
platform	платформа	*pluttforma*
play	пьеса	*pyessa*
play	играть	*eegrart*

play golf	играть в гольф	*eegrart vgorlf*
playground	детская площадка	*dyetskaya plushchartka*
playing cards	(игральные) карты	*(eegrarlny-yeh) karty*
pleasant	приятный	*preeyartny*
please	пожалуйста	*puzharlooysta*
pleasure	удовольствие	*ooduvvorlstviyeh*
plum	слива	*sleeva*
pocketknife	складной нож	*skluddnoy norsh*
point (vb)	показать	*pukkuzzart*
poison	яд	*yart*
police	милиция	*meeleetsiya*
police station	отделение	*utdilyayniyeh*
	милиции	*meeleetsii*
policeman	милиционер	*mileetseeonyair*
pond	пруд	*proot*
pony	пони	*porni*
pop concert	поп-концерт	*popkuntsairt*
population	население	*nussilyayniya*
pork	свинина	*sveeneena*
port (drink)	портвейн	*purrtvayn*
porter	носильщик	*nusseelshchik*
porter	швейцар	*shvaytsar*
post	почта	*porchta*
post code	почтовый индекс	*porchtorvy eendeks*
postage	почтовый сбор	*porchtorvy zbor*
postbox	почтовый ящик	*puchtorvy yashchik*
postcard	открытка	*utkrytka*
postman	почтальон	*porchtalyorn*
potato	картофель	*kartorfil*
poultry	птица	*pteetsa*
powdered milk	порошковое	*purushkorvoyeh*
	молоко	*mullukkor*
power point	розетка	*ruzzyetka*
pram	детская коляска	*dyetskaya kullyarska*
prawns	креветки	*krevvyetki*
precious	дорогой	*durruggoy*
prefer	предпочесть	*pridpuchayst*

preference	предпочтение	*pridpuchtyayniyeh*
pregnant	беременная	*biryayminnaya*
present	присутствующий	*preesootstvooyushchi*
present	подарок	*puddaruk*
preserves	варенье	*varyaynyeh*
press (vb)	нажать	*nuzhart*
pressure	давление	*duvvlyayniyeh*
price	цена	*tsinar*
price list	указатель цен	*ookuzzartyel tsen*
print (vb)	печатать	*pichartat*
print	отпечаток	*utpichartuk*
probably	наверно	*nuvvyairna*
problem	проблема	*prubblyema*
profession	профессия	*pruffaysseeya*
programme	программа	*pruggrarma*
pronounce	произнести	*pruh-eeznisstee*
propane camping gas	пропан	*prupparn*
pudding	пудинг	*poodink*
pull	удалить	*oodulleet*
pull a muscle	растянуть мышцу	*rasstyannoot myshtsoo*
pulse	пульс	*poolss*
punctually	во время	*vorvraymya*
puncture	лопнула шина	*lorpnoola shina*
pure	чистый	*cheesty*
purple	лиловый	*leelorvy*
purse	кошелёк	*kushilyok*
push	толкать	*tulkart*
puzzle	головоломка	*gulluvvalormka*
pyjamas	пижама	*peezharma*

Q

quarter	четверть	*chaytvirt*
quarter of an hour	четверть часа	*chaytvirt chussar*
queen	королева	*kurrullyevva*
question	вопрос	*vupprorss*
quick	быстрый	*bystry*
quiet	спокойный	*spukkoyny*

R

radio	радио	*rahdeeo*
railway	железная дорога	*zhilyeznaya durrorga*
rain	дождь	*dorsht*
raincoat	плащ	*plarshch*
raining	идёт дождь	*eedyot dorsht*
raisins	изюм	*eezyoom*
rape	изнасилование	*eeznusseeluvvarneeyeh*
rapids	быстрина	*bystrinar*
raspberries	малина	*mulleena*
raw	сырой	*syroy*
raw ham	ветчина	*vitchinnar*
raw vegetables	сырые овощи	*syry-yeh orvushchi*
razor blades	(бритвенные)	*(breetvinny-yeh*
	лезвия	*lyayzviya*
read	читать	*chitart*
ready	готовый	*guttorvy*
really	собственно	*sorpstvinna*
receipt	квитанция	*kveetarntsiya*
receipt	справка	*sprarfka*
	(об уплате)	*(ubb ooplartyeh)*
receipt	чек	*chyek*
recipe	рецепт	*ritsept*
reclining chair	шезлонг	*shezlornk*
recommend	рекомендовать	*rekummyenduvvart*
rectangle	прямоугольник	*pryarmmuh-oogorlnik*
red	красный	*krarssny*

red wine	красное вино	*krarsnoyeh veenor*
reduction	скидка	*skeetka*
refrigerator	холодильник	*khulludeelnik*
regards	привет	*preevyet*
region	область	*orblust*
registered	заказной	*zukkuzznoy*
reliable	надёжный	*nuddyozhny*
religion	религия	*releegiya*
rent out	сдать (внаём)	*zdart (vnayom)*
repair (vb)	починить	*puchinneet*
repairs	ремонт	*rimornt*
repeat	повторить	*pufturreet*
report	протокол	*pruttukkorl*
resent	обижаться	*ubbeezhartsa*
responsible	ответственный	*utvyetstvunny*
rest	отдохнуть	*utdukhnoot*
restaurant	ресторан	*risturrarn*
result	результат	*ryezooltart*
retired	пенсия	*pyensiya*
retired	на пенсии	*nah pyensii*
return (ticket)	(билет) туда и обратно	*(beelyet) toodar ee ubbrartno*
reverse (vehicle)	ехать задним ходом	*yekhat zardnim khordum*
rheumatism	ревматизм	*rivmutteezm*
rice	рис	*reess*
ridiculous	ерунда	*yiroondar*
riding (horseback)	ездить на лошади	*yezdeet nah lorshudi*
riding school	манеж	*munnyesh*
right	правый	*prarvy*
right (on the)	направо	*nupprarva*
right of way	преимущество	*prayimooshchistva*
ring (on telephone)	позвонить	*puzzvunneet*
ripe	зрелый	*zryelly*
risk	риск	*reesk*
river	река	*rikkar*
road	дорога	*durrorga*

roadway	дорога	*dur**or**ga*
roasted	жареный	*zhar**inn**y*
rock	скала	*skul**lar***
roll	булочка	*b**oo**luchka*
roof rack	империал	*eempere**earl***
room	комната	*k**or**mnutta*
room number	номер	*n**or**mer*
room service	обслуживание в	*ubbsl**oo**zhivarniyeh*
	номере	*vn**or**meryeh*
root	корень	*k**or**in*
rope	верёвка	*vir**yo**ffka*
rose	роза	*r**or**za*
rosé wine	розовое вино	*r**or**zuvvoyeh veen**or***
roundabout	площадь с	*pl**or**shchud*
	круговым	*skr**oo**guvvym*
	движением	
route	маршрут	*marshr**oot***
rowing boat	гребная лодка	*gribn**ah**ya l**or**tka*
rubber	резина	*rye**zee**na*
rubbish	ерунда	*yir**oo**ndar*
rucksack	рюкзак	*ry**oo**kzark*
rude	невежливый	*nyehv**yay**zhlivy*
ruins	развалины	*ruzv**ar**leeny*
run into	встретить	*fstr**ay**teet*

S

sad	грустный	*gr**oo**sny*
safari	сафари	*suf**far**i*
safe	безопасный	*byezupp**ar**ssny*
safe	сейф	*sayf*
safety pin	английская булавка	*ungl**ee**skaya bool**ar**fka*
sail (vb)	плавать	*pl**ar**vat*
sailing boat	парусная лодка	*par**oo**snaya l**or**tka*
salad	салат	*sul**lart***
salad oil	растительное	*rast**ee**tyelnaya*
	масло	*m**ar**sslo*

salami	салями	*sullyarmi*
sale	распродажа	*russpruhdarzha*
salt	соль	*sorl*
same	то же самое	*tor zhe sarmoyeh*
sandy beach	песчаный пляж	*pishcharny plyash*
sanitary pad	гигиеническая	*geegeeyeneech*
	прокладка	*eskaya prukklartka*
sardines	сардины	*sardeeny*
satisfied	довольный	*duvorlny*
Saturday	суббота	*sooborta*
sauce	соус	*sor-ooss*
sauna	сауна	*sahoona*
sausage	колбаса	*kullbussar*
savoury	солёный	*sullyony*
say	сказать	*skuzzart*
scarf	шарф	*sharf*
scenic walk	прогулка по городу	*pruggoolka puh goruddoo*
school	школа	*shkorla*
scissors	ножницы	*norzhneetsy*
scooter	мотороллер	*muttaroriler*
scorpion	скорпион	*skurpeeorn*
Scotland	Шотландия	*shuttlarndiya*
Scots (adj)	шотландский	*shutlarnski*
Scotsman	шотландец	*shuttlarndits*
Scotswoman	шотландка	*shuttlarntka*
screw	винт	*veent*
screwdriver	отвёртка	*utvyortka*
sculpture	скульптура	*skoolptoora*
sea	море	*moryeh*
seasick	его укачало	*yivvor ookucharla*
seasoning	приправа	*preeprarva*
seat	место	*myesta*
second (n)	секунда	*sikkoonda*
second	второй	*fturroy*
secretion (of fluid etc)	выделение	*vydelyayniye*
sedative	успокаивающее	*uspukkaheevay*
	средство	*ooshchiye sraytstva*

203

see	осматривать	*usmartreevart*
self-timer	автоспуск	*ufftaspoosk*
send	отправить	*uttprarveet*
sentence	предложение	*pridluzhayniyeh*
September	сентябрь	*sintyarbr*
serious	серьёзный	*siryozny*
service	обслуживание	*ubsloozhivarniyeh*
serviette	салфетка	*sulfyetka*
set (hair)	сделать завивку	*zdyelart zuvveefku*
sewing thread	швейные нитки	*shvayny-yeh neetkee*
shade	тень	*tyen*
shallow	мелкий	*myelki*
shammy	замша	*zarmsha*
shampoo	шампунь	*shampoon*
shark	акула	*ukkoola*
shave (vb)	побрить	*pubbreet*
shaver	электробритва	*ellektrobreetva*
shaving cream	крем для бритвы	*kryem dlya breetyah*
shaving soap	мыло для бритвы	*mylo dlya breetyar*
sheet	простыня	*prustynyah*
sherbet	шербет	*shirbyet*
sherry	херес	*khay-ress*
shirt	рубашка	*roobarshka*
shoe	туфля	*tooflya*
shoe polish	гуталин	*gootulleen*
shoe repairs	ремонт обуви	*rimornt orboovi*
shoe shop	обувной магазин	*ubboovnoy mugguzzeen*
shoelace	шнурок	*shnoorork*
shop (vb)	делать покупки	*dyelat pukoopki*
shop	магазин	*mugguzzeen*
shop assistant	продавщица	*pruddafshcheetsa*
shop window	витрина	*vitreena*
shopping centre	торговый центр	*turrgorvy tsentr*
short	короткий	*kurrortki*
short circuit	короткое	*kurrortkoyeh zum*
	замыкание	*mykarniyeh*
shorts	шорты	*shorty*

shoulder	плечо	*plichor*
show	шоу	*shoroo*
shower	душ	*doosh*
shutter	затвор	*zuttvor*
sieve	решето	*rishittor*
sign (vb)	подписать	*puddpeessart*
sign	дорожный знак	*durrorzhny znark*
signature	подпись	*portpeess*
silence	тишина	*tishinar*
silver	серебро	*siribror*
silver-plated	посеребрённый	*pussirribryonny*
simple	простой	*prustoy*
single (berth)	одноместный	*udnamyestny*
single (of journey)	в один конец	*vuddeen kunnyets*
single	неженатый (незамужняя)	*nyehzhinarty (nye hzumoozhnyaya)*
single	холостяк	*khullustyark*
sir	господин	*gusspuddeen*
sister	сестра	*syistrar*
sit	сидеть	*seedyayt*
size	размер	*razmyair*
ski (vb)	кататься на лыжах	*kuttartsa nah lyzhakh*
ski boots	лыжные ботинки	*lyzhny-yeh butteenki*
ski goggles	лыжные очки	*lyzhny-yeh uchkee*
ski instructor	инструктор по лыжному спорту	*eenstrooktur puh lyzhnummoo*
ski lessons/class	занятіfl по лыжному катанию	*zunnyartiya puh lyzhnummoo*
ski lift	(лыжный) подъёмник	*(lyzhny) puddyomnik*
ski pants	лыжные брюки	*lyzhny-yeh bryooki*
ski slope	горнолыжная трасса	*gornolyzhnaya trarssa*
ski stick	лыжная палка	*lyzhnaya parlka*
ski suit	лыжный костюм	*lyzhny kustyoom*
ski wax	лыжный воск	*lyzhny vorsk*
skimmed	полужирный	*pulloozheerny*

skin	кожа	*korzha*
skirt	юбка	*yoopka*
skis	лыжи	*lyzhi*
sleep (vb)	спать	*spart*
sleeping car	спальный вагон	*sparlny vuggorn*
sleeping pills	снотворные	*snuttvorny-yeh*
	таблетки	*tubblyetki*
slide	слайд	*slight*
slip	комбинация	*kumbinartsiya*
slip road	подъезд	*pudd-yest*
slow	медленный	*myedlinny*
slow train	пассажирский	*pussazheerski*
	поезд	*por-yist*
small	маленький	*marlinki*
small change	мелочи	*myeluchi*
smell	вонять	*vunnyart*
smoke	дым	*dym*
smoke	курить	*kooreet*
smoked	копчёный	*kupchony*
smoking compartment	купе для	*koopeh dlya*
	курящих	*kooryahshchikh*
snake	змея	*zmeeya*
snorkel	шноркель	*shnorkyil*
snow (vb)	идёт снег	*eedyot snyek*
snow	снег	*snyek*
snow chains	цепь	*tsep prutteevoskul*
	противоскольжения	*lzhayniya*
snug	уютный	*ooyootny*
soap	мыло	*myla*
soap box	мыльница	*mylnitsa*
soap powder	стиральный	*steerarlny*
	порошок	*purrushork*
soccer (to play)	играть в футбол	*eegrart ffootborl*
soccer match	футбольный мяч	*fooborlny myach*
socket	розетка	*ruzzyetka*
socks	носки	*nusskee*

soft drink	прохладительный напиток	*prukhludd**ee**tyelny n**uppee**tuk*
sole (of shoe)	подошва	*pudd**or**shva*
sole (fish)	морской язык	*murrsk**oy** yuzz**yk***
solicitor	адвокат	*udvukk**art***
someone	кто-то	*kt**or**-tuh*
something	что-то	*sht**or**-tuh*
sometimes	иногда	*eenugd**ah***
somewhere	где-то	*gd**yeh**-ta*
son	сын	*syn*
soon	скоро	*sk**ora***
sore	нарыв	*nar**yff***
sore throat	боль в горле	*borl vg**or**lye*
sorry	извини(те)	*eezveen**ee(tyeh)***
sort	сорт	*sort*
soup	суп	*soop*
sour	кислый	*k**ee**sly*
sour cream	сметана	*smitt**ar**na*
source	источник	*eest**or**chnik*
south	юг	*yook*
souvenir	сувенир	*soovinn**eer***
spaghetti	спагетти	*spugg**ye**ti*
spanner	вилочный ключ	*v**ee**luchny klyooch*
spanner	гаечный ключ	*g**igh**-yechny klyooch*
spare	запас	*zupp**arss***
spare part	запчасть	*zuppch**arst***
spare parts	запчасти	*zuppch**arsti***
spare tyre	запасная шина	*zuppuss**nah**ya shina*
spare wheel	запасное колесо	*zuppuss**noryeh** kulliss**or***
speak	говорить	*guvvurr**eet***
special	особенный	*uss**or**byuny*
specialist	специалист	*spetsial**eest***
specialty	специальность	*spetsi**ar**lnust*
speed limit	максимальная скорость	*makseem**ar**lnaya sk**or**ust*
spell out	сказать по буквам	*skuzz**art** puh b**oo**kvum*
spicy	пикантный	*peek**arn**tny*

splinter	заноза	*zunn**or**za*
spoon	ложка	*l**or**shka*
sport (to play)	заниматься спортом	*zunnim**ar**tsa* *sp**or**tom*
sport	спорт	*sport*
sports centre	спортивный зал	*spurrt**ee**vny zarl*
spot	место	*m**yes**ta*
sprain	вывихнуть	*vyvikhnoot*
spring	весна	*visn**ar***
square	площадь	*pl**or**shchad*
square	квадратный	*kvudd**rar**tny*
square metres	квадратный метр	*kvudd**rar**tny myetr*
squash (to play)	играть в сквош	*eegr**ar**t fskv**or**sh*
stadium	стадион	*studdee**orn***
stage	сцена	*s-ts**en**na*
stain	пятно	*pyitn**or***
stain remover	пятновыводитель	*pyitnovyvudd**ee**tyel*
stairs	лестница	*l**yay**snitsa*
stalls	зал	*zarl*
stamp	марка	*m**ar**ka*
starch	крахмал	*krukhm**arl***
start	завести	*zuvvist**ee***
station	вокзал	*vukkz**arl***
statue	памятник	*p**ar**myutnik*
stay	остановиться	*ustunnuv**ee**tsa*
stay	остаться	*ust**ar**tsa*
stay	пребывание	*prebyv**ar**niyeh*
steal	украсть	*ookr**ar**st*
steel	сталь	*starl*
stench	вонь	*vorn*
sting	жалить	*zh**ar**leet*
stitch (medical)	шов	*shorf*
stitch (vb)	сшить	*s-sheet*
stockings	чулки	*choolk**ee***
stomach	желудок	*zhil**oo**duk*
stomach ache (he has)	у него болит живот	*oo nivvor bull**eet** zhiv**ort***
stomach ache	боль в желудке	*borl vzhil**oo**tkyeh*

stomach cramps	колики	*korleeki*
stools	испражнение	*eespruzhnyayniyeh*
stop (vb)	остановить	*ustunnuvveet*
stop	остановка	*ustunnorfka*
stopover	промежуточная посадка	*prummizhootuch naya pussartka*
storey	этаж	*etarzh*
storm (vb)	бушевать	*booshivart*
storm	буря	*boorya*
straight	прямой	*pryummoy*
straight ahead	прямо	*pryarmo*
straw	соломинка	*sullorminka*
strawberries	клубника	*kloobneeka*
street	улица	*oolitsa*
strike (n)	забастовка	*zubbustorfka*
strong	крепкий	*kryepki*
study (vb)	учиться	*oocheetsa*
stuffing	начинка	*nucheenka*
subscriber's number	номер телефона	*normer tyeliforna*
subtitled	с субтитрами	*s-soopteetrummi*
succeed	удаться	*oodartsa*
sugar	сахар	*sarkhar*
suit	костюм	*kustyoom*
suitcase	чемодан	*chimmuddarn*
summer	лето	*lyeta*
summertime	летнее время	*lyetnyeyeh vraymya*
sun	солнце	*sorntsa*
sun hat	шляпа от солнца	*shlyappa ut sorntsa*
sunbathe	загорать	*zuggurrart*
Sunday	воскресенье	*vusskrissyaynyeh*
sunglasses	тёмные очки	*tyomny-yeh uchkee*
sunrise	восход солнца	*vusskhort sorntsa*
sunset	заход солнца	*zakkhort sorntsa*
sunstroke	солнечный удар	*sorlnyechny oodar*
suntan lotion	крем для загара	*kryem dlya zuggara*
suntan oil	масло от солнечных ожогов	*marssla ut sorlnyechnykh uzhorguff*

supermarket	универсам	*ooneevyairs**arm***
surcharge	доплата	*duppl**arta***
surf (vb)	заниматься	*zunneem**arts**a*
	серфингом	*sy**air**fingum*
surf board	доска для	*dusk**ar** dlya*
	серфинга	*sy**air**finga*
surgery	приёмные часы	*pree**yo**mny-yeh chuss**y***
surname	фамилия	*fam**ee**liya*
surprise	сюрприз	*syoorpr**ee**ss*
swallow	проглотить	*pruggluttee**t***
swamp	болото	*bull**orta***
sweat (n)	пот	*port*
sweet	конфетка	*kunf**ye**tka*
sweet (adj)	сладкий	*sl**ar**tki*
sweetcorn	кукуруза	*kookoor**oo**za*
sweeteners	таблетки сахарина	*tubbl**yet**ki sukhar**ee**na*
sweets	конфеты	*kunf**ye**tty*
swim	плавать	*pl**ar**vat*
swimming bath attendant	инструктор	*eenstr**oo**ktur*
swimming pool	бассейн	*buss**yay**n*
swimming trunks	плавки	*pl**ar**fki*
swindle (n)	жульничество	*zh**oo**lnichestsva*
switch	выключатель	*vyklyooch**ar**tyel*
synagogue	синагога	*seenugg**or**ga*

T

table	стол	*storl*
table tennis (to play)	играть в	*eegr**art** vnust**or**lny*
	настольный теннис	*t**e**nnees*
tablet	таблетка	*tubbl**yet**ka*
take (of time)	длиться	*dl**ee**tsa*
take (photograph)	фотографировать	*futtagruff**ee**ruvvat*
take	принять	*preeny**art***
taken	занятый	*z**ar**nyaty*
talcum powder	тальк	*tarlk*
talk	говорить	*guvurr**ee**t*

tampons	тампон	*tumporn*
tanned	загорелый	*zagurryelly*
tap	кран	*krarn*
tap water	водопроводная вода	*vuddupruvvordnaya vuddar*
taste (vb)	попробовать	*pupprorbuvvart*
tax free shop	магазин беспошлинной торговли	*mugguzzeen bye sporshleenoy turrgorvli*
taxi	такси	*tukksee*
taxi stand	стоянка такси	*stuyahnka tukksee*
tea	чай	*chigh*
teapot	чайник	*chighnik*
teaspoon	чайная ложка	*chighnaya lorshka*
teat (on bottle)	соска	*sorska*
telegram	телеграмма	*tyeligrarma*
telephoto lens	телеобъектив	*tyeli-ubb-yekteef*
television set	телевизор	*tyeliveezur*
telex	телекс	*tyeleks*
temperature	температура	*tyemperutoora*
temporary filling	временная пломба	*vrayminnaya plormba*
tender (meat)	мягкий	*myakhki*
tennis (to play)	играть в теннис	*eegrart ftenniss*
tennis ball	теннисный мяч	*tennissny myach*
tennis court	теннисная площадка	*tennissnaya plushchartka*
tennis racket	теннисная ракетка	*tennissnaya rukkaytka*
tenpin bowling	играть в кегли	*eegrart fkyegli*
tent	палатка	*pullartka*
tent peg	колышек	*korlyshek*
terrace	терраса	*tyairarssa*
terrible	ужасно	*oozharssna*
terribly	чрезвычайно	*chryayzvychighno*
thank	благодарить	*bluggadurreet*
thank you	спасибо	*spasseeba*
thanks	спасибо	*spasseebo*
thaw (vb)	таять	*tahyart*

theatre	театр	*tee-artr*
theft	кража	*krarzha*
there	там	*tarm*
thermal bath	термическая ванна	*tyairmeecheskaya varna*
thermometer	термометр	*tyairmormyetr*
thick	толстый	*torlsty*
thief	вор	*vorr*
thigh	бедро	*byidror*
thin	тонкий	*tornki*
thin	худой	*khoodoy*
things	вещи	*vyayshchi*
think	думать	*doomat*
third (n)	треть	*tryet*
thirst	жажда	*zharzhda*
this afternoon	сегодня днём	*sivvordnya dnyom*
this evening	сегодня вечером	*sivvordnya vyaychirum*
this morning	сегодня утром	*sivvordnya ootrum*
thread	нитка (ниточка)	*neetka (neetuchka)*
thread	нить	*neet*
throat	горло	*gorla*
throat lozenges	таблетки для горла	*tubblyetki dlya gbla*
throwing up	меня рвёт	*minya rvyort*
thunderstorm	гроза	*gruzzar*
Thursday	четверг	*chitvyairk*
ticket (admission)	билет	*beelyet*
ticket (travel)	билет	*beelyet*
tickets	билеты	*beelyety*
tidy	убрать	*oobrart*
tie	галстук	*garlsstuk*
tights	колготки	*kulgortki*
time	время	*vraymya*
times	раз	*rarss*
timetable	расписание	*rasspeessarniye*
tin	банка	*barnka*
tip	на чай	*nah chigh*
toast	тост	*torst*
tobacco	табак	*tubbark*

tobacconist's shop	табачная лавка	*tubbarchnaya larfka*
toboggan (n)	сани	*sarni*
today	сегодня	*sivvordnya*
toe	палец	*parlyets*
together	вместе	*vmyestyeh*
toilet	туалет	*too-ullyet*
toilet paper	туалетная бумага	*too-uhlyetnaya boomarga*
toiletries	туалетные	*too-uhlyetny-yeh*
	принадлежности	*preenuddlyezhnusti*
tomato	помидор	*pummeedor*
tomato purée	томатное пюре	*tummartnoyeh pyooray*
tomato sauce	(томатный) кетчуп	*(tummartny) kyetchoop*
tomorrow	завтра	*zarftra*
tongue	язык	*yuzzyk*
tonic water	тоник	*tornik*
tonight	сегодня ночью	*sivvordnya norchyoo*
too much	слишком много	*sleeshkum mnorga*
tools	инструменты	*eenstroomyenty*
tooth	зуб	*zoop*
toothache	зубная боль	*zoobnahya borl*
toothbrush	зубная щётка	*zoobnahya shchotka*
toothpaste	зубная паста	*zoobnahya parsta*
toothpick	зубочистка	*zoobocheestka*
top up	дополнить	*dupporlneet*
total	общий	*orbshchi*
tough	жёсткий	*zhostki*
tour	прогулка	*pruggoolka*
tour guide	гид	*geet*
tourist card	туристическая	*tooreesteecheskaya*
	карта	*karta*
tourist class	туристский класс	*tooreestski klarss*
Tourist Information Office	туристическое бюро	*tooreesteecheskoyeh byooror*
tourist menu	меню для туристов	*minyoo dlya tooreestuff*
tow (vb)	взять на буксир	*vzyart nah bookseer*
tow cable	буксир	*bookseer*
towel	полотенце	*pullutyentseh*

tower	башня	*barshnya*
town hall	ратуша	*rartoosha*
town city	город	*gorut*
toy	игрушка	*eegrooshka*
traffic	движение	*dveezhayniyeh*
traffic light	светофор	*svyetafor*
train	поезд	*por-yist*
train ticket	билет (на поезд)	*beelyet (nah por-yist)*
train timetable	расписание	*russpeessarniyeh*
	поездов	*puh-yizdorff*
training shoes	кроссовки	*krussorfki*
translate	перевести	*pirivisstee*
travel (vb)	путешествовать	*pootyeshestvvuvvart*
travel agent	бюро путешествий	*byooror pootyeshestviy*
travel guide	путеводитель	*pootyevuddeetyel*
traveller	путешественник	*pootyeshestvennik*
traveller's cheque	дорожный чек	*durrorzhny chyek*
treacle/syrup	патока	*partukka*
treatment	лечение	*lichayniye*
tree	дерево	*dyayrivva*
triangle	треугольник	*tray-oogorlnik*
trim	подстричь	*puddstreech*
trip	экскурсия	*ekskoorseeya*
trip	путешествие	*pootyeshestviyeh*
trip	поездка	*puhyestka*
troubled by	его беспокоит	*yivor byespukkor-eet*
trousers	брюки	*bryooki*
trout	форель	*furrel*
trunk call	междугородный	*myezhdoogurrordny*
trunk code	код (города)	*kort (gorudda)*
trustworthy	надёжный	*nuddyozhny*
try on	примерить	*preemyaireet*
tube	тюбик	*tyoobik*
Tuesday	вторник	*ftornik*
tumble drier	сушилка	*soosheelka*
tuna	тунец	*toonyets*
tunnel	туннель	*toonel*

turn	раз	*rahss*
TV	телевизор	*tyeliveezur*
TV and radio guide	программа радио-	*pruggrarma*
	и телепередач	*rahdeeo- ee*
tweezers	пинцет	*peentset*
tyre	покрышка (шины)	*pukkryshka (shiny)*
tyre lever	монтажная	*muntarzhnaya lup-*
	лопатка для шин	*partka dlya shin*

U

umbrella	зонтик	*zorntik*
under	под	*pudd*
underground	метро	*myitror*
underground railway system	сеть метрополитена	*syayt myitruppullitayna*
underground station	станция метро	*starntsiya mitror*
underpants	трусы	*troossy*
understand	понять	*punnyart*
underwear	нижнее бельё	*neezhnyeyeh billyor*
undress	раздеть	*ruzzdyayt*
unemployed	безработный	*byezrubbortny*
uneven	неровный	*nyehrorvny*
university	университет	*ooneevairsityayt*
unleaded	без свинца	*byes sveentsah*
up	наверх	*nuvvyairkh*
urgency	поспешность	*pusspyeshnust*
urgent	срочный	*srorchny*
urine	моча	*muchar*
use	использовать	*eessporlzuvvart*
usually	чаще всего	*charshcher vsivvor*

vacate	освободить	*ussvubbudeet*
vaccinate	привить	*preeveet*
vagina	влагалище	*vluggarleeshcheh*
vaginal infection	влагалищная	*vluggarleeshch*
	инфекция	*naya eenfyektseeya*
valid	действующий	*dyaystvooyushchi*
valley	долина	*dulleena*
valuable	дорогой	*durrugoy*
van	фургон	*foorgorn*
vanilla	ваниль	*vunneel*
vase	ваза	*varza*
vaseline	вазелин	*vazilleen*
veal	телятина	*tilyartina*
vegetable soup	овощной суп	*uvvushchnoy soop*
vegetables	овощи	*orvushchi*
vegetarian	вегетарианец	*vegeturreeahnyets*
vehicle documents	технический	*tyekhneecheski*
	паспорт	*parsspurt*
vein	вена	*vyenna*
venereal disease	венерическая болезнь	*vyenereecheskaya bullyezn*
vermin	вредители	*vrideetyeli*
via	через	*chayruss*
video recorder	видеомагнитофон	*videeomuggneetufforn*
video tape	видеоплёнка	*videeoplyonka*
view	вид	*veet*
village	деревня	*dirayvnya*
visa	виза	*veeza*
visit	посетить	*pussiteet*
visit	гости	*gorsti*
vitamin tablets	таблетки витамина	*tubblyetki veetummeena*
vitamins	витамины	*veetummeeny*
vodka	водка	*vortka*
volcano	вулкан	*voolkarn*
volleyball	играть в волейбол	*eegrart v vullayborl*
vomit	рвать	*r-vart*

wait	ждать	*zhdart*
waiter	официант	*uffitsiarnt*
waiting room	зал ожидания	*zarl uzhidarniya*
waitress	официантка	*uffitsiarntka*
wake up	разбудить	*ruzzboodeet*
Wales	Уэльс	*Oo-ellss*
walk (n)	прогулка	*prugoolka*
walk	гулять	*goolyart*
wallet	бумажник	*boomarzhnik*
wardrobe	гардероб	*gardyirorp*
warm	тёплый	*tyoply*
warn	предупредить	*pridooprideet*
warning	предупреждение	*pridooprizhdyayn iyeh*
wash (clothes)	стирать	*steerart*
washing-powder	моющее средство	*mor-yooshchiyeh sryetstva*
washing	бельё	*bilyor*
washing line	бельевая верёвка	*bilyevahya viryofka*
washing machine	стиральная машина	*steerarlnaya mushina*
wasp	оса	*ussar*
water	вода	*vuddar*
water melon	арбуз	*arbooss*
water ski (vb)	кататься на водных лыжах	*kuttartsa nah vordnykh lyzhakh*
waterproof	водонепрониц-аемый	*vuddanyehprunnitsahye my*
wave-pool	бассейн с искусственными волнами	*bussayn skoostvinnymi*
way	средство	*sraytstva*
we	мы	*my*
weak	слабый	*slarby*
weather	погода	*puggorda*
weather forecast	прогноз погоды	*prugnorss puggordy*
wedding	свадьба	*svardba*

Wednesday	среда	*sriddar*
week	неделя	*nidyaylya*
weekend	выходные (дни)	*vykhuddnyyeh (dnee)*
weekend duty	в эти выходные	*vehti vykhudnyyeh*
	он работает	*orn rubortayeht*
weekly ticket	абонемент на	*abbunnimyent nah*
	неделю	*nidyaylyu*
welcome	добро пожаловать	*dubbror puzharluvvat*
well (advb)	хорошо	*khurushor*
Welsh (adj)	валлийский	*vulleesski*
Welshman	валлиец	*vulleeyets*
Welshwoman	валлийка	*vulleeka*
west	запад	*zarput*
wet	мокрый	*morkry*
wetsuit	костюм для	*kustyoom dlya*
	серфинга	*syairfinga*
what is the problem?	на что вы	*na shtor vy*
	жалуетесь?	*zharlooyetyes?*
what?	что?	*shtor?*
wheel	колесо	*kullissor*
wheelchair	инвалидное кресло	*eenvulleednuhyeh kraysla*
when?	когда?	*kugdar?*
where?	где?	*gdyeh?*
which?	какой?	*kukkoy?*
whipped cream	взбитые сливки	*vzbeety-yeh sleefki*
white	белый	*byely*
who?	кто?	*ktor?*
wholemeal	из муки грубого	*eess mookee groobuvva*
	помола	*pummorla*
wholemeal bread	хлеб грубого	*khlyep groobuvva*
	помола	*pummorla*
why?	почему?	*puchimoo?*
wide-angle lens	широкоугольный	*shirorka-oogorlny*
	объектив	*ubbyekteef*
widow	вдова	*vduvvar*
widower	вдовец	*vduvvyets*
wife	жена	*zhinnar*

wild strawberries	земляника	*zimlyuneeka*
wind	ветер	*vyaytyer*
windbreak	ветровой щит	*vitruvvoy shcheet*
windmill	мельница	*myelneetsa*
window	окно	*uknor*
windscreen wiper	дворник	*dvornik*
wine	вино	*veenor*
wine list	меню алкогольных	*minyoo ullkuggorl*
	напитков	*nykh nuppeetkuff*
winter	зима	*zeemar*
witness	свидетель	*svidyaytyel*
woman	женщина	*zhenshchinna*
wool	шерсть	*shairst*
word	слово	*slorva*
work	работа	*rubborta*
working day	рабочий день	*rubborchiy dyen*
worn	поношенный	*punnorshunny*
worried (to be)	волноваться	*vullnuvvartsa*
wound	рана	*rarna*
wrap	завернуть	*zuvvirnoot*
write	писать	*peessart*
write down	записать	*zuppeessart*
writing pad	блокнот	*blukknort*
writing paper	почтовая бумага	*puchtorvaya boomarga*
written	письменный	*peesmunny*
wrong	неправильный	*nyeh-prarveelny*

Y

yacht	яхта	*ya**rkh**ta*
year	год	*go**rt***
yellow	жёлтый	*zh**o**lty*
yes	да	*dah*
yes please	с удовольствием	*sooduvv**orl**stviyem*
yesterday	вчера	*vchir**ar***
yoghurt	кефир	*kyeff**eer***
you	вы	*vy*
you too	вам того же	*varm tuvv**or** zheh*
youth hostel	молодёжная турбаза	*mullud**yo**zhnaya turb**ar**za*

Z

| zip | молния | *m**or**lneeya* |
| zoo | зоопарк | *zuh-uhp**ark*** |

Basic grammar

1 The importance of suffixes, and their varying forms

There are no *the* and *a/an* words in Russian. Thus **дом** (dorm) can mean 'the house', 'a house', or plain 'house'. Prefixing the noun with **этот/тот** (etut/tort – this/that) is often useful: **этот/тот дом** (etut/tort dorm – this/that house).

Russian has three genders: masculine, feminine and neuter. As a rule, nouns that end in a consonant are masculine, e.g. **чемодан** (chimma**darn** – a suitcase); nouns ending in **-a** or **-yah** are feminine, e.g. **девушка** (dy**ay**vooshka – a girl) and **тётя** (ty**o**tya – aunt); nouns ending in **-o** or **-yeh** are neuter, e.g. **окно** (ukkn**or** – window) and **море** (m**o**ryeh - sea).

Adjectives must agree in gender with the nouns they go with:

masculine adjectival ending **-ый** (**-y**) or **-ой** (**-oy**), therefore **красивый дом** (kruss**ee**vy dorm – beautiful house), **молодой человек** (mull**u**ddoy chillovy**e**k – young man);

feminine adjectival ending **-ая** (**-aya**), therefore **красивая девушка** (kruss**ee**vaya dy**ay**vooshka – beautiful girl);

neuter adjectival ending **-oe** (**-or-yeh**), therefore **красивое море** (kruss**ee**vor-yeh m**o**ryeh – beautiful sea).

In the plural there is a single form **-ые** (**y-yeh**) for all genders:

красивые дома (kruss**ee**vy-yeh dumm**ar** – beautiful houses)
красивые девушки (kruss**ee**vy-yeh dy**ay**vooshki – beautiful girls)
красивые моря (kruss**ee**vy-yeh murr**ya** – beautiful seas)

2 Nouns

Much of the complexity of Russian derives from the fact that nouns, pronouns and adjectives also change according to which of six 'cases' (nominative, accusative, genitive etc.) they are in, and according to gender and number – far too intricate for a basic grammar!

In this phrasebook it is generally the masculine form that is given, but wherever necessary the feminine form is also given in brackets. This is especially necessary when you are using the past tense, which is basically a form of the verb ending in 'l':

я был	*ya byl*	I (a man) was
я прочитал	*ya pruchitarl*	I (a man) have read
я была	*ya bylah*	I (a woman) was
я прочитала	*ya pruchitarla*	I (a woman) have read
это было	*ettuh bylo*	it (a thing) was
море было	*moryeh bylo*	the sea (neuter noun) was.

3 Vowel harmony

In other words, in the past the verb ends in '**l**' for masculine singular, '**-la**' for feminine singular, and '**-lo**' for neuter singular. For the plural there is one ending, '**-lee**':

мы были	*my bylee*	we were

In the present, Russian does not use a verb 'to be'. Thus **он врач** (*orn vrarch* - he doctor) means 'he is a doctor', and **она красивая девушка** (*unnah krusseevaya dyayvooshka* - she beautiful girl) means 'she is a beautiful girl'. To say 'I am' etc, you need just the pronouns:

я	*ya*	I (am)
ты	*ty*	you (informal form) (are)
он/она/оно	*orn/unnah/unnor*	he/she/it (is)

мы	*my*	we (are)
вы	*vy*	you (formal/plural) (are)
они	*unnee*	they (are)

The verb 'to have' is rendered by a prepositional construction meaning roughly 'there is about me':

у меня есть	*oo minyah yest*	I have
у тебя есть	*oo tibbyah yest*	you (informal form) have
у него есть	*oo nyivvor yest*	he has
у неё есть	*oo nyeeyor yest*	she has
у него есть	*oo nyivvor yest*	it has

у нас есть	*oo narss yest*	we have
у вас есть	*oo varss yest*	you (formal/plural) have
у них есть	*oo neekh yest*	they (masc/fem/neut) have